Knights on the Prairie: A History of Templary in Oklahoma

By
Trasen Solesmont Akers

Copyright © 2012 by Trasen S. Akers. All rights reserved.

No part of this publication may be reproduced, stored in a retrieval system or transmitted in any way by any means, electronic, mechanical, photocopy, recording, or otherwise without the prior permission of the author.

A portion of the proceeds from the sale of this work will benefit the Oklahoma Knights Templar Holy Land Pilgrimage Fund.

Published in the United States of America

ISBN: 978-1-105-99932-1

First edition: August 2012

Sir Knight James C. Taylor
1929 – 2011

Dedication

This work is dedicated to the Sir Knights past and present who have diligently worked to see that the torch of Templary is never extinguished; but more especially, this work is dedicated to the late Sir Knight James C. Taylor, Past Department Commander. Those who knew him called him Jim and the Eminent Sir Knight embodied all that was Templary.

Jim graduated from Oklahoma A&M in 1951 with a degree in Animal Husbandry. He would go onto serve two years with the 3rd Infantry Division in Korea and was discharged as a 1st Lieutenant.

Jim was raised to the Sublime Degree of Master Mason in Roosevelt Lodge No. 398 AF&AM in Roosevelt, Oklahoma. It was on July 5, 1956, that he was dubbed and created a Knight of the Temple. For Jim, Templary was in his blood as his Father, John I. Taylor, was elected Grand Commander in 1939. Jim would go onto serve as Commander of Elk City Commandery No. 22 in 1965 and 1966.

Prior to being elected to the progressive line of the Grand Commandery of Oklahoma in 1968 as Eminent Grand Warder, Jim served as Captain of the State-Wide Drill Team. He was able to reprise this role again in 2009 as the Grand Commandery paraded for the Centennial of the Most Worshipful Grand Lodge of the State of Oklahoma. Jim was elected Grand Commander in 1974 and in time would take a seat on the Work & Tactics Committee, faithfully teaching and preserving the ritualistic work of the Order.

In 1994 Jim was appointed Right Eminent Department Commander for the South Central Department of the Grand

Encampment of Knights Templar of the United States. After his tenure in this office ended, Jim continued to faithfully serve the Grand Commandery of Oklahoma and Templary in general until his death in 2011.

Sir Knight James C. Taylor's presence will certainly be missed by the Sir Knights of Oklahoma. His dedication will always be remembered and his lasting mark upon the Order will be ever present.

Contents

Acknowledgements iii
Foreword v

I: Two Sisters 1

II: Prosperity Abounds 33

III: Dark Days 61

IV: Decline and Renewal 85

Appendix A – Commanderies Chartered 111
Appendix B – Grand Commander Portraits 117
Appendix C – Past Grand Officers 187
Appendix D – Knights Templar Cross of Honor 193
Appendix E – Masonic Papers of Note 197

Acknowledgements

There are countless people without whom Historians would be unable to bring to light events of bygone eras. In this regard I am no exception and I am deeply indebted to those who follow.

To Mrs. Applegate and Mr. Thompson; thank you for cementing in me a desire for the written word and the preservation of our History.

To William A. "Pete" Nation, I. Dwayne Dixon, Robert T. Shipe, and Lewis A. Hullum; thank you for believing in me and helping me to grow in York Rite Masonry.

To Steven P. Guerrero, Clyde H. Schoolfield, and Robert G. Davis; thank you for your friendship and wise counsel with this endeavor.

To my wife Aeriel; thank you for tolerating my mental absence these past few months and keeping such a brave face while becoming a "Masonic Widow" at a young age.

Finally, to my Mother and Father; without your undying love this work, and every other challenge I have tackled in life, would not have been possible.

While a number have helped with this project, any errors that appear are solely my own.

Foreword

By Steven P. Guerrero, Jr.

As I read the following pages in this text, one word kept coming to my mind. The word was HONOR. That particular word means several different things to several different people. Our ancient brethren surrendered their lands, titles, and claims to all assets for the HONOR of being dubbed and created a Knight Templar. The vocation of protecting Christian Pilgrims within the Holy Land was bestowed upon them, and they accepted the challenge with faith and HONOR.

In modern times Sir Knights have also had to give up something of tremendous value in our daily lives. The valuable asset in which I speak is time. Within this book you will see that the generations before us have put forth considerable time and effort to learn and practice their ritual. They also had to invest countless hours to perfect drill teams in order to compete and succeed at a State and National level.

Within these pages you will also read about various decisions the Grand Commandery of Oklahoma and the Grand Commandery of Indian Territory have had to make over the years. One of the more important decisions was to merge the two Grand Commanderies into one. Since the merger we see the Grand Commandery of Oklahoma flourish and flounder at different times throughout history. There has however, always been one constant within our beloved Oklahoma Grand Commandery. It has always been a great HONOR to be called an Oklahoma Knights Templar. We owe a tremendous debt to the Templars who have come before us, and likewise we have an equally tremendous legacy to pass on to the future Oklahoma Knights Templars that will come after us.

A special thank you goes to the author of this book. It is truly an HONOR to have a small part in such an important Oklahoma Knights Templar literary work.

I: Two Sisters

Some Historians have noted that, in comparison to neighboring states such as Texas, the history of Oklahoma can be somewhat dry. Those who have the privilege of calling Oklahoma home know that one need only scratch the surface to discover a truly colorful history. The story of Oklahoma is one of Indians, outlaws, cowboys, and Freemasons. Throughout the history of what would eventually become the State of Oklahoma, one can readily find the influence of Freemasonry. Early military operations in Indian Territory brought Brethren to the frontier at places such as Fort Gibson, numerous statesmen of the Five Civilized Tribes would come to take the Degrees of Freemasonry, and when statehood finally came to be, the Fraternity was well represented at the Oklahoma Constitutional Convention. As Freemasonry thrived in the bustling Territories, so came all the trappings of fraternalism. One of those trappings that would come to prominence was that of the Knights Templar and the early history of the Knights Templar in Oklahoma is, much like that of the State itself, a tale of two sisters.

It could easily be said that wherever civilization spreads, Freemasonry soon follows; the United States is no exception in this regard. It is believed that the birthplace of Masonic teachings in America was at Tun Tavern in Philadelphia in 1731.[1] This was followed by the reprinting of Anderson's *Constitutions of the Free-Masons* by Benjamin Franklin in 1734.[2] As Freemasonry gained speed in the colonies, it was not uncommon for "higher" or side degrees to be conferred in addition to the three degrees of the Symbolic Lodge. The two more prevalent of these additional degrees were that of the Holy Royal Arch and the Order of the Temple. The earliest recorded conferral of the Order of the

Temple was within St. Andrews Lodge in Boston on August 28, 1769. It is believed that the ritual for the degree was provided by members of the various military lodges of the British Army then stationed in the area. Templary in America was loosely practiced from then on until the Grand Encampment of Knights Templar of the United States was formally organized in 1816.[3]

As the young nation began to move west, so did Freemasonry. By the 1820s the southwestern border of the United States reached to Fort Smith, Arkansas. In order to protect the border, Colonel Matthew Arbuckle established Fort Gibson in 1824 at the confluence of the Grand and Arkansas Rivers. After the Indian Removal Act of 1830 the post would take on a peace keeping role between the Plains Indians and the Five Civilized Tribes who came to call the new Indian Territory home. The placement of Fort Gibson proved to be a detriment to the Army as the post flooded often and many a soldier died of disease; but the post was in relative proximity to Tahlequah, capital of the Cherokee Nation, and Park Hill, home to several leading Cherokee statesmen.[4] On November 9, 1848, a charter was granted to Cherokee Lodge No. 21 at Tahlequah by the Grand Lodge of Arkansas F&AM and thus Freemasonry officially arrived in the Indian Territory.[5] Between 1850 and 1855, Lodges were charted at Fort Gibson, Doaksville, Stilwell, and the Creek Agency.[6] When war erupted in 1861, the Indian Territory was not spared its ravages. The Lodges located in Indian Territory became dormant during the Civil War and the lack of reports to the Grand Lodge of Arkansas led to the belief that all of the Indian Territory charters had been destroyed in the War.[7] This belief was not true though as Joseph Coody of Muscogee Lodge No. 93 (present day Eufaula Lodge No. 1) carried the Lodge Charter throughout his service with the Confederate Army and immediately upon cessation of hostilities, with George W. Stidham, resumed Masonic activities; though now at Eufaula and not the Creek Agency.[8]

While a major event in the history of the United States, the American Civil War was a minor setback for Freemasonry in what would become Oklahoma. All of the original Lodges operating in Indian Territory would ultimately be re-chartered after the war and new Lodges came into existence. One of those new Lodges was

Oklahoma Lodge No. 217 at Boggy Depot, I.T.[9] A leading force behind the Masonic activity at Boggy Depot was the Reverend Joseph Samuel Murrow.[10] A Southern Baptist Missionary who also served as a Confederate Indian Agent during the Civil War, Murrow became acquainted with Freemasonry through his friend General Albert Pike during their service with the Confederacy.[11] Murrow took the degrees of Freemasonry in 1867 in Andrew Jackson Lodge No. 88 of Linden, Texas. He then demitted to Oklahoma Lodge No. 217 on February, 16, 1867.[12] Murrow would serve as the second Grand Master of the Grand Lodge of Indian Territory and held the office of Grand Secretary for thirty years.[13] In 1880 Murrow was dubbed and created a Knight of the Temple at Coeur de Leon Comandery No. 17 in Parsons, Kansas.[14] It would be another ten years before a Commandery of Knights Templar was officially formed in the region but it is safe to say that the Order was gaining attention.[15]

The Land Run of 1889 opened up what was known as the Unassigned Lands to settlement and the Oklahoma Territory was established in the summer of 1890.[16] Those who came to settle the new territory also brought with them Freemasonry. Before the territorial government could even be established a charter was granted to Guthrie Lodge No. 35 on November 6, 1889, by the Grand Lodge of Indian Territory. Shortly thereafter, Lodges residing in Oklahoma Territory established their own Grand Lodge.[17] A cursory reading of the proceedings of the Grand Commandery of Oklahoma shows there were groups of Templars residing in the region holding memberships in other jurisdictions; one of these early groups just so happened to settle in Guthrie after the Land Run of 1889. The summer of 1890 was a very busy summer indeed; in addition to the creation of the territorial government, a group of twenty Sir Knights in Guthrie petitioned the Grand Encampment of Knights Templar of the United States to open a Commandery of Knights Templar on July 12, 1890.[18] Guthrie Commandery No. 1 was granted a dispensation to work with Cassius M. Barnes at the helm; Barnes would go on to serve as the Fourth Territorial Governor of Oklahoma.[19]

The proceedings for the 1892 Triennial of the Grand Encampment show that Templary was gaining momentum in the sister territories that would become the State of Oklahoma. Both

Rev. Joseph S. Murrow
Courtesy of the Grand Chapter of Royal Arch Masons of Oklahoma

Honorary Past Grand Commander Jewel of Joseph S. Murrow
Courtesy of Robert G. Davis

Muskogee Commandery No. 1 in Indian Territory and Oklahoma Commandery No. 2 at Oklahoma City in Oklahoma Territory received dispensations to work during this period, each with seventeen and sixteen Sir Knights respectively.[20] To institute the Commandery at Muskogee, a group of Sir Knights from Parsons, Kansas, some of whom had probably been at the Knighting of Reverend Murrow, journeyed to Indian Territory by way of a special train on the M.K.T. Railway in the Autumn of 1891.[21] The next two years saw the creation of three more Commanderies in the region. In Oklahoma Territory, Ascension Commandery No. 3 was established at El Reno on May 8, 1893. In Indian Territory, Chickasaw Commandery No. 2 at Purcell was established on May 31, 1894, and McAlester Commandery No. 3 at McAlester on July 14, 1894.[22] With three Commanderies each now residing in the two territories, the ground work was laid for the creation of Grand Commanderies.

The formation of the first Commandery at Guthrie was by all means an experiment, as Masonic bodies can whither and die on the vine. The expedient growth of Templary in those early years in the territories shows that there was a strong desire for the Chivalric Degrees in the region. In a move that certainly added to the initial success, the Grand Lodge of Indian Territory in 1890 recognized the formation of a Commandery in their jurisdiction. Further securing legitimacy for the Order, the Grand Lodge recognized the Grand Encampment as the legal occupant of Indian Territory and stated that no degrees of Knighthood other than those of the Grand Encampment and the Ancient and Accept Scottish Rite were legitimate.[23] It was in Indian Territory that the idea for a Grand Commandery was first proposed. On December 27, 1895, a convention was held in Muskogee, I.T., for the purpose of forming a Grand Commandery. Under a special warrant given by Most Excellent Grand Master Warren LaRue Thomas of the Grand Encampment, Muskogee Commandery No. 1, Chickasaw Commandery No. 2, and McAlester Commandery No. 3 assembled and formed the Grand Commandery of Knights Templar of the Indian Territory. The new Grand Commandery was instituted by Very Eminent William H. Mayo Grand Recorder of the Grand Encampment with the following officers being elected and appointed:

Grand Commander: Robert W. Hill

Deputy Grand Commander: James E. Humphrey

Grand Generalissimo: Edmond H. Doyle

Grand Captain General: Patrick J. Byrne

Grand Senior Warden: Alfred D. Hawk

Grand Junior Warden: Daniel M. Hailey

Grand Prelate: William P. Paxson

Grand Treasurer: James J. McAlester

Grand Recorder: Leo E. Bennett

Grand Standard Bearer: Zachary T. Walrond

Grand Sword Bearer: Joseph S. Childs

Grand Warder: William E. Hailey

Grand Captain of the Guard: Benjamin L. Robertson

Grand Sentinel: Stephen Becker

Drill Master and Inspector: James A. Scott[24]

Seal of the Grand Commandery of the Indian Territory

And so began the Grand Commandery of Indian Territory as the forty-first Grand Commandery to be established by the Grand Encampment.[25] Her neighbors to the west were taking note of the goings on in Indian Territory and she would soon have a younger sister.

Those early Royal Arch Masons in the newly created Oklahoma Territory sought their dispensations to work from the Grand Chapter of Indian Territory, which had been created in November of 1890. As such, that Grand Chapter was able to establish supremacy in the region and no Grand Chapter was ever established in Oklahoma Territory.[26] The situation for those Sir Knights in Oklahoma Territory wishing to commence work on their own was inherently different. The Grand Encampment of Knights Templar of the United States holds jurisdiction over all Templary in the United States. In the absence of a Grand Commandery in a territorial jurisdiction, charters are granted to subordinate Commanderies of the Grand Encampment.[27] On November 8, 1895, Grand Master Thomas granted a special warrant to those Commanderies in Oklahoma Territory to form a Grand Commandery in the same fashion as Indian Territory.[28] It is due to this allegiance to a national governing body that sister Grand Commanderies came to be in the twin territories. Though the Sir Knights of Indian Territory were the proverbial "Sooners" in the run to establish a Grand Commandery, a conclave was called at Guthrie on February 10, 1896, for the purpose of establishing such a Grand Body. With Cassius M. Barnes acting as proxy for Grand Master Thomas, representatives of Guthrie Commandery No. 1, Oklahoma Commandery No. 2, and Ascension Commandery No. 3 duly formed the Grand Commandery of Oklahoma. The "lateness" of this action was apparently due in part to Ascension No. 3 not being properly instituted, an issue that was rectified shortly after being brought to Grand Master Thomas' attention.[29]

In the creation of the Grand Commandery of Oklahoma, Cassius M. Barnes was once again at the helm. Having been the charter Commander of Guthrie Commandery No. 1, his fellow Sir Knights of Oklahoma Territory placed their trust in him as their first Grand Commander. It also appears that in a show of union, the Deputy Grand Commander, Grand Generalissimo, and Grand Captain General were each elected from Oklahoma, Ascension, and Guthrie Commanderies respectively. Those first grand officers were as follows:

Grand Commander: Cassius M. Barnes

Deputy Grand Commander: DeForest D. Leach

Grand Generalissimo: Otto A. Schuttee

Grand Captain General: William S. Spencer

Grand Senior Warden: Benjamin E. Binns

Grand Junior Warden: Fred S. Goodrich

Grand Prelate: Angus G. Crockett

Grand Treasurer: Luke Ellison

Grand Recorder: Harper S. Cunningham

Grand Standard Bearer: Fred S. Goodrich

Grand Sword Bearer: Edward S. Donnelly

Grand Warder: Charles A. Morris

Grand Captain of the Guard: William J. Pettee[30]

Seal of the Grand Commandery of Oklahoma

Barnes was not only a leading Mason in Oklahoma Territory, but he was also a leading citizen. As previously noted, he became the Fourth Territorial Governor but prior to that he served in the Union Army during the Civil War, was Chief Deputy of the US Marshals at Fort Smith, Arkansas, was appointed Receiver of the United States Land Office in Guthrie, was Speaker of the House of the Third Territorial Legislature, and after serving as Territorial Governor became Mayor of Guthrie.[31] Upon the forming of the Grand Commandery of Oklahoma, Barnes gave a stirring address of which included these remarks:

We seek to join together in bonds that are more sacred and binding if possible than any other can be, those who have proven themselves by terms of pilgrimage and warfare through the degrees of the ancient craft; who have wrought in the quarries and brought forth good specimens of their skill in the Masonic art, and who have by successfully traveling rough and rugged roads arrived at high eminence in the Royal Arch, and by their patience and perseverance, their constancy, courage, and fortitude have demonstrated their capacity and fitness to be clothed as princes of the royal household.

The newly formed Grand Commandery of Oklahoma, its work complete, adjourned for the day with a combined membership of 131 Sir Knights.[32] With the 43rd Grand Commandery now established, Templary in the twin territories was quickly becoming an Order of prominence.[33]

By 1897 the two Grand Commanderies were just beginning to find their footing. The 1896 proceedings of Indian Territory show active fraternal correspondence with other jurisdictions in addition to the acknowledgment of the formation of the Grand Commandery of Oklahoma. Further solidifying this fraternal bond was the presence of the Deputy Grand Commander of Oklahoma, DeForest Leach, at the conclave of Indian Territory.[34] What can probably be considered the main purpose of a Grand Commandery is the dissemination of Templary in their jurisdiction. Both Grand Commanderies immediately took up the banner by chartering new Commanderies right away. Before the century would close, Oklahoma chartered St. Johns Commandery No. 4 at Stillwater in 1897.[35] The Sir Knights of Indian Territory also chartered two new Commanderies during this period, though this was not done without incident. At this time in order for a new Commandery to receive a dispensation to work they were required to obtain the blessing of a neighboring Commandery. In 1896 Sir Knights in Chickasha had a desire to form a Commandery and the nearest Commandery to them happened to be Chickasaw No. 2 at Purcell. Unfortunately due to the proximity of Chickasha to Purcell, the Sir Knights of Purcell refused to give their consent to forming a Commandery at Chickasha. It would take intervention by the Committee on

Sir Knights and Officers of the Grand Commandery of Oklahoma assembled at Guthrie in 1902

Courtesy of Oklahoma Commandery No. 3

Charters and Dispensations, but DeMolay Commandery No. 4 was ultimately chartered at Chickasha.[36] The following year a similar situation arose when Ardmore attempted to establish a Commandery. Again Purcell opposed the formation of a new Commandery within proximity of them and it was believed that a Commandery at Ardmore would destroy Purcell. Though the Committee on Charters and Dispensations was not in favor of a Commandery at Ardmore, Grand Commander James E. Humphrey granted them a charter in 1897.[37]

The turn of the century would see seventeen Commanderies established in Oklahoma prior to 1912 and nine in Indian Territory.[38] It is evident by these numbers that Templary was spreading like a wildfire across the prairies of Oklahoma Territory. Like in Indian Territory, the Sir Knights of Oklahoma were not immune to opposition when seeking to form a new Commandery. In 1905 Sir Knights at Frederick petitioned for a dispensation to work. To their dismay it was the opinion of the Grand Commandery "that it would be bad precedent to establish weak Commanderies in small towns with populations of less than 700."[39] The following year Grand Commander W.J. Pettee of Oklahoma made a point of noting in his address that new Commanderies were being formed without jealousy of others. He even answered the request of the Sir Knights at Frederick and granted them a charter as Frederick Commandery No. 13.[40] The year 1905 also saw a charter granted to Ada Commandery No. 6, though again not without opposition from Purcell.[41] As if in an effort to tell the Sir Knights of Purcell to be more receptive to the growth of the Order, the Twelfth Conclave of Indian Territory was held in the Asylum of the newly chartered Ada Commandery No. 6.[42]

It was in the fall of 1907 that the two territories would be merged into the State of Oklahoma, but for the Sir Knights in the region the bulk of the year was business as usual. Oklahoma chartered an additional four Commanderies without incident with the exception of Emmanuel No. 16 at Blackwell. The Committee on Charters and Dispensations was of the opinion that establishing another Commandery in Kay County would cripple Ponca City. Fortunately for the Sir Knights in Blackwell, Grand Commander C.P. Wickmiller rejected the report and granted the

Grand Officers of Oklahoma in 1905

Courtesy of the Grand Commandery of Oklahoma

charter.[43]   After a few years without chartering any new Commanderies, Indian Territory sprang to life in 1908. It was as if they saw the proverbial hand writing on the wall and seven of the fourteen Commanderies in existence in Indian Territory prior to 1912 were established.[44]

In the late 1800s the Grand Encampment officially standardized the ritual of the Order but the tactics, the ritual used to open a meeting, used by each Grand Jurisdiction varied. This variance was so great in Indian Territory that it was noted that each Commandery was using their own tactics, leading to the first discussions on establishing uniform tactics for the opening ceremonies.[45] The 1898 Proceedings of Indian Territory show that Grand Commander Edmond Doyle made a further attempt to rectify the ritualistic differences by issuing General Order No. 4 which established annual inspections of the constituent Commanderies. The order lacked teeth though as these "inspections" were essentially visits by the Grand Commander or his Representative to be certain that each Commandery was operating as it should be.[46] Ultimately, it was becoming quite clear to the powers that be that a "serious lack of military discipline" existed within the Commanderies of Indian Territory. This resulted in a call for more detailed inspections with the constituent Commanderies being required to pay the expenses of the Inspecting Officer.[47] Charles Creager took note of this "discipline issue" in his seminal work on Freemasonry in Oklahoma and said the following in regards to a cornerstone ceremony:

> …there were only fourteen complete uniforms in Muskogee at the time but it was very important that the Commandery make an "excellent showing" so it was decided to divide the uniforms and equipment among as many as possible on the theory that the more men there were in line, the more good it would do the Commandery. As a result, when the lines were formed for the parade, some of the "valiant heroes" had ten-gallon Stetsons and some had chapeaux… But it was a "complete" success and the opinion prevailed that the "high Masons looked grand."[48]

This was not the only discussion on uniforms in Indian Territory. Apparently there was a growing trend among Past Commanders to purchase expensive and elaborate uniforms that were not regulation. Grand Commander Frank Smith ordered this to stop and while he may have curbed such future purchases it is likely those with said uniforms continued to wear them.[49] A similar situation concerning tactics existed in Oklahoma, but after careful study of the tactics of surrounding Jurisdictions, the Sir Knights moved to adopt the tactics of Missouri in 1904.[50]

The year 1904 is also worth noting for another ritual issue in Oklahoma, this time regarding missing rituals themselves. At this point in Templary in America rituals were highly regulated and printed in code. Of the Grand Officers, only four were granted rituals by the Grand Encampment. These officers were the Grand Commander, the Deputy Grand Commander, the Grand Generalissimo, and the Grand Captain General. By 1904 the Grand Commander's assigned ritual had apparently gone missing and it was believed to be held by Stillwater. Grand Commander Enoch Bamford demanded that Stillwater relinquish the ritual but when Stillwater was refused a replacement by the Grand Encampment, it became quite clear that this was not the missing ritual.[51] Ultimately the ritual issue was resolved, but the Sir Knights quickly learned they must keep a better accounting of their assigned rituals. It was during the 10th Annual Conclave of Oklahoma that the Committee on Work & Tactics was established thus bringing regulation in earnest to the ritual.[52]

One of the grand characteristics of Templary is that of charity and while both Grand Commanderies were still in their infancy, they each found time to exercise this characteristic. In 1900 what would be a category four hurricane struck Galveston, Texas, and the call for donations went out; Indian Territory responded with $300 for the relief effort.[53] A few short years later in 1905 the town of Snyder, Oklahoma, was devastated by what would today be considered an F5 tornado. The death toll was officially estimated at 111 or twelve percent of the population.[54] The Sir Knights of Oklahoma voted to send $50 for the relief of Sir Knights residing in Snyder; the Commanderies at Lawton, Hobart, and Fredrick drew members from the area.[55] The following year, San Francisco would experience the "Great Quake of 1906" and the call went out for aide. The Sir Knights of Oklahoma saw fit to send a total of $270 for the relief of the Sir Knights of San Francisco.[56] Indian Territory also answered this call and another of a more local nature. Past Grand Commander John Coyle had lost everything he owned in a fire, including his Knights Templar uniform. In honor of his service, the Grand Commandery purchased Coyle a new uniform.[57] In 1911 both Grand Commanderies provided funds for fire apparatus at the Masonic Home that had been established at the Darlington Agency near present day El Reno.[58] Though at times there was little in the coffers, as illustrated by the Treasurer's Report at the 1896 conclave of Indian Territory which showed a balance of $3.05, charity was practiced as often as possible by those early Sir Knights.[59]

Membership, as it is today, has always been a point of concern for Grand Commanders attempting to navigate the murky waters of the Order's existence. Grand Commander Zachary T. Walrond of Indian Territory observed that only one in four Royal Arch Masons had pursued the Orders of Templary. Walrond went on to state that every Sir Knight should attend their Chapter regularly as "the work is far superior to any fraternity that is not Masonic."[60] There was also a growing problem with Sir Knights letting their memberships in the Lodge and Chapter lapse. Per the rules of the Grand Encampment, such lapse was to result in a Sir Knight being deprived of his membership in the Commandery if it continued for six months.[61] The travel required for many Masons likely factored into their ability to pursue the Orders of Templary. Private automobile travel was a luxury at this time and travel of any distance had to be undertaken by train. In an effort to promote attendance at the 1907 conclave of Oklahoma, the session was held in conjunction with the state meeting of the Jewelers Association so that the Sir Knights could benefit from the discounted rail fares.[62] A scattered membership and "sojourning" Sir Knights, or those living in the Jurisdiction with memberships elsewhere, was viewed as a problem in Indian Territory. In an effort to remedy this it was suggested that those Sir Knights residing in Indian Territory with memberships elsewhere be denied visitation, this was however not adopted.[63] This "sojourning" was best illustrated in 1906 when Paris Commandery No. 9 of Texas requested a dispensation to participate in a cornerstone ceremony on the state line. The following telegram was received from Grand Commander

Harwood of Texas, to which Grand Commander Coyle gave his consent:

> John Coyle, Rush Springs, IT: Dispensation granted Paris Commandery No. 9 to act as escort to Hugo Lodge in laying corner stone March 14, subject to your permission to invade Territory.
>
> T.F. Harwood[64]

It is likely that several of these Sir Knights holding membership in Texas were residing on the northern bank of the Red River. Oklahoma also had its share of "sojourning" Sir Knights and in 1910 a group residing near Waurika requested dispensation to appear in uniform for a Christmas celebration with the local Lodge. These Sir Knights not being members of Oklahoma but Kansas, Texas, and Missouri, Grand Commander Edward P. Gallup denied the request.[65]

In addition to the assorted committee reports and official actions of each Grand Commandery, the proceedings provide a glimpse into the general goings on of Templary in the Territories. For example, at the 8th Annual Conclave of Indian Territory in 1902 the Grand Commandery briefly adjourned during their session to parade through the streets of McAlester.[66] A few short years later in 1906, McAlester Commandery No. 3 escorted the Grand Lodge at a cornerstone ceremony for their own Knights Templar building on Grand Avenue in downtown McAlester.[67] In 1903 the Grand Commandery of Oklahoma purchased a complete set of Grand Officer Jewels, which are still in use today.[68] Several notables in Oklahoma history were also actively involved with Templary. It was in 1902 that Sir Knight Edwin DeBarr of Oklahoma Commandery No. 2 served as Grand Prelate.[69] DeBarr was one of the four original faculty members of the University of Oklahoma and established the Chemistry and Chemical Engineering Departments in addition to the School of Pharmacy.[70] In April of 1907 James B.A. Robertson was installed as Junior Warden at Chandler; Robertson would later serve as Governor of Oklahoma.[71]

Along with the success of the Order, the proceedings also report the trials incident to human life that the Sir Knights faced.

Knights Templar Building on Grand Avenue in McAlester, Oklahoma

Courtesy of Steve DeFrange

McAlester Commandery No. 3 at 1906 Independence Day Parade

Courtesy of Steve DeFrange

A common setback in those early days was fire. By 1897 Sir Knights at Purcell had already suffered two fires.[72] Shortly after being constituted, Ardmore Commandery No. 5 was ravaged by fire.[73] A fire at the Capitol Printing Office in Oklahoma resulted in the destruction of the only copy of the 1902 proceedings. Fortunately for the Sir Knights of Oklahoma, Grand Recorder Harper S. Cunningham was able to recreate the work from memory.[74] In 1908 the Sir Knights of Pawnee Commandery No. 7 lost all of their paraphernalia to a fire. In an effort to allow them to rebuild, the Grand Commandery of Oklahoma remitted the dues for those Sir Knights at Pawnee.[75] While all of these losses were devastating in their own right, none eclipsed the fire that ravaged the Masonic Temple in Muskogee on February 23, 1899. The loss was estimated at $6,000 but the insurance that had been purchased only provided for $3,000 in coverage. It was believed that the brick structure at Muskogee was fireproof, this turned out not to be the case and all of the Grand Commandery of the Indian Territory's records were lost. Reacting to this, Grand Recorder Joseph S. Murrow constructed a special archive for future records at his home near Atoka.[76]

A review of the inspection reports of Oklahoma for 1910 really underscores the previously mentioned issues that the Sir Knights faced. Weatherford No. 11 noted that many of their Sir Knights did not reside close enough to attend meetings regularly. Enid No. 8 was observed as having been "quiet for a number of years" and that they were in need of "youth and vigor." The report of Lawton No. 12 also mentioned a lack of attendance but stated that they had the best arranged and finest equipped Asylum in the State. Pawnee No. 7 was still recovering from the recent fire but their newly installed officers performed the Order of the Temple in its entirety. The inspection of Hobart No. 10 had twenty-six Sir Knights in attendance with all but two in uniform. The Sir Knights of Elk City No. 15 had been working without any copies of the tactics for opening and were completely unsure of the floor work; the Grand Recorder quickly saw this issue remedied. It was noted that Oklahoma No. 2 was the largest Commandery in the state but due to the number of Sir Knights who had affiliated from other Jurisdictions, their ritual and uniforms were "not quite regular." Perry No. 5 was the smallest

Pawnee Commandery No. 7 in the early 1900s
Courtesy of the Oklahoma Historical Society

Commandery in the State at this time but they had eight "teams" of Masons pursuing the Chapter degrees, all of which were expected to become Knights Templar. The Sir Knights at Ascension No. 3 were meeting in their newly completed Temple which had accommodations expressly for the Order of the Temple. The inspection report notes the following:

> A novel feature in the construction of the Asylum was the Chamber of Reflection which was placed in an adjoining room west of the Asylum and perhaps five feet above the floor of the Asylum. There was an adjustable door connecting the Chamber of Reflection and the Asylum which at the proper time could be opened after the lights in the Asylum had been extinguished. Thus enabling the Sir Knights within the Asylum to view the actions of the candidate while he in turn could see nothing in the Asylum.

At Frederick No. 13, twenty-five Sir Knights gathered for the Inspection. In an effort to promote participation, they allowed no candidate to receive the Orders of Templary until their uniform had arrived.[77]

Every three years the Grand Encampment of Knights Templar of the United States holds its Triennial Conclave. While the annual conclaves of the Grand Commandery were the main events of Templary in the territories, the Triennial Conclave was the main event of Templary in the Nation. Both Grand Commanderies made certain to send delegations to the Triennial regularly with Indian Territory sending her first delegation to Pittsburg in 1898.[78] In 1907 Grand Commander Henry K. Ricker of Oklahoma journeyed to Saratoga Springs with the Grand Commandery of Kansas by way of special train. Upon arrival, he found himself outnumbered by a six man delegation from Indian Territory. Ricker noted that the entire town was decorated with banners of the Order and electric lights illuminated the skies at night. He was honored with the position of mounted aide to Sir Knight Sol E. Waggoner, Chief of the 10th Division in the parade which consisted of 15,000 Sir Knights.[79]

As the Sir Knights marched through the years that marked the turn of the century, the merging of the two territories into one state was ever present in their minds and this is also meant that the time would ultimately come for the two Grand Commanderies to consolidate. In 1906 Oklahoma sent a delegation to attend the Annual Conclave of Indian Territory to discuss uniting the two Jurisdictions.[80] Indian Territory had authorized a similar delegation in 1905 to discuss the matter with Oklahoma.[81] Unfortunately the merging of the two territories into one government had still not been set into motion. Grand Commander John Coyle of Indian Territory notes this inaction for unification by Washington in his 1906 address with the remark "Alas, poor Congress."[82] It was in 1907 that statehood became a reality and the twin territories were combined into one.[83] Grand Commander Ricker of Oklahoma discussed consolidation of the two Grand Commanderies in his 1908 address and had the following to say:

> We are now a State with two Grand Bodies within our borders, and in my judgment that ought not to prevail and one that should be met with an earnest purpose to promote the welfare of our beloved Order in this new State.[84]

It was also in 1908 that the Sir Knights of Indian Territory held a Special Conclave to discuss consolidation, Most Excellent Grand Master Henry H. Rugg of the Grand Encampment was even present in anticipation of consolidation. Unfortunately it was all for not as the vote for consolidation was thirty-six for and twenty-two against. With such a strong minority, Grand Master Rugg chose not to continue with consolidation for the time being.[85]

A total of 26,000 Sir Knights attended the Triennial of the Grand Encampment in 1910 at Chicago, Illinois. Most Excellent Grand Master Rugg who had only recently been in Oklahoma to facilitate consolidation urged the Grand Commanderies of Oklahoma and Indian Territory to consolidate but chose to leave it to the Grand Commanderies to arrange.[86] In a letter to Grand Commander Fuller of Oklahoma, the newly elected Grand Master William B. Melish stated that it would give him great pleasure to hear of steps being taken for consolidation and that he hoped to receive news of such steps while traveling in England. While the tone of the letter was certainly pleasant, such correspondence from the supreme authority of Templary in the United States was without question an ultimatum.[87] It was on April 21, 1911, while in conclave at Chickasha that some sixty-five members of Indian

1910 Grand Commandery of Oklahoma Triennial Attendance
Jewel

Courtesy of T.S. Akers

Territory assembled and voted in favor of consolidation. In order to commence with consolidation the two Grand Commanderies were to convene in Oklahoma City on October 6, 1911; this would require Indian Territory to obtain a dispensation from Grand Master Melish to assemble outside of her jurisdiction.[88] Both Grand Commanderies met at the Skirvin Hotel and formed in procession at nine in the morning headed by Sir Knight Orin Ashton mounted on a white steed with the Knights Templar band immediately behind him. The Sir Knights then marched to the "Baptist White Temple" located at 400 North Broadway in Oklahoma City.[89] Once all the remaining business of the Grand Commanderies was settled, Grand Master Melish declared the Grand Commandery of Indian Territory "closed without day forever."[90] Immediately following Indian Territory surrendering her charter was the election of officers for the consolidated Grand Commandery. The Grand Commander was to be elected from what comprised Indian Territory, the Deputy Grand Commander from Oklahoma, and so on down the line. The first Grand Officers of the consolidated Grand Commandery of Oklahoma were as follows:

    Grand Commander: Robert H. Henry

    Deputy Grand Commander: Guy W. Bohannon

    Grand Generalissimo: William H. Essex

    Grand Captain General: John A. Gillis

    Grand Senior Warden: James A. Scott

    Grand Junior Warden: James Q. Louthan

    Grand Prelate: Joseph S. Murrow

    Grand Treasurer: Ira B. Kirkland

    Grand Recorder: George W. Spencer

    Grand Standard Bearer: Fred H. Smith

    Grand Sword Bearer: Eugene P. McMahon

    Grand Warder: Edward W. Gilfillan

    Grand Sentinel: Fred H. Clark

In the spirit of Brotherly Love it was decided that the next conclave of the Grand Commandery of Oklahoma would be held

The Four Oldest Past Commanders of Indian Territory in 1911
Courtesy of the Grand Commandery of Oklahoma

L to R: James E. Humphrey, Daniel M. Hailey, Edmond H. Doyle, and James A. Scott

in Muskogee, formerly located in Indian Territory. For the first time in the history of the Grand Encampment of Knights Templar of the United States, two Grand Commanderies joined as one. Outgoing Grand Commander John R. Hamill made the following remarks concerning the merger in his address:

> ...Sir Knights of both jurisdictions we have, heretofore, marched along the highway in parallel columns, now let us march along in a single column and we will continue to grow in Templar Masonry until we of time set a votive stone that the memory of consolidation may remain with us vivid as it is this moment, so that when like our sires, we are gone, our sons will sing our praises in memory of this deed redeemed.

And thus two Grand Commanderies were united as one with a combined membership of 1,932 Sir Knights.[91]

The "Baptist White Temple" at 400 North Broadway in Oklahoma City

Courtesy of T.S. Akers

Present day marker at the site of the "Baptist White Temple" in Oklahoma City

Courtesy of T.S. Akers

Inscription Reads: This marker is placed as nearly as possible to the location of the southwest corner of the renowned White Temple, a structure that served the community in many civic capacities until razed in 1926 for construction of the local office of the Western Union Telegram Company. Erected in 1905 as the First Baptist Church, it then was acquired by India Temple and later by the Masonic Bodies. The name was due to the color of the exterior.

Notes

[1] Henry W. Coil, "Introduction of Freemasonry into America," *Coil's Masonic Encyclopedia* (Richmond: Macoy Publishing & Masonic Supply Co., 1961), 31-33.

[2] "Pennsylvania Masonic History," The Grand Lodge of Free and Accepted Masons of Pennsylvania, <http://www.pagrandlodge.org/programs/masedu/qa/41-50.html>, Accessed 25 March 2012.

[3] Frederick G. Speidel, *The York Rite of Freemasonry: A History and Handbook* (Mitchell-Fleming Printing Inc., 1978), 53.

[4] "Fort Gibson," Oklahoma Historical Society's Encyclopedia of Oklahoma History and Culture, <http://digital.library.okstate.edu/encyclopedia/entries/F/FO033.html>, Accessed 25 March 2012.

[5] Charles E. Creager, *History of Freemasonry in Oklahoma* (Muskogee, Oklahoma: Muskogee Print Shop, 1935), 20.

[6] Raymond L. Holcomb, *Father Murrow: The Life and Times of Joseph Samuel Murrow, Baptist Missionary, Confederate Indian Agent, Indian Educator, and the Father of Freemasonry in Indian Territory* (Atoka County Historical Society, 1994), 105.

[7] "A Brief History of Cherokee Lodge #10," Cherokee Lodge #10, <http://www.leftmoon.com/cherokee10/history.asp>, Accessed 25 March 2012.

[8] "Eufaula Masonic Lodge: Oldest in Oklahoma," *The Indian Journal*, 2 March 1922, p. 3.

[9] Creager, 38.

[10] "Fraternal Orders," Oklahoma Historical Society's Encyclopedia of Oklahoma History and Culture, <http://digital.library.okstate.edu/encyclopedia/entries/F/FR007.html>, Accessed 25 March 2012.

[11] Bobby L. Ellenwood, "Southern Baptists in Oklahoma Masonry," *Transactions of the Texas Lodge of Research* (Waco, Texas: 1996), Vol. XXX.

[12] William R. Denslow, *10,000 Famous Freemasons* (Richmond: Macoy Publishing & Masonic Supply Co., 1957), Vol. 3: 249-250.

[13] Ellenwood.

[14] Holcomb, 105.

[15] Grand Encampment of Knights Templar of the United States, *Proceedings of the 25th Triennial Conclave* (Richmond: Wm. Ellis Jones, Book and Job Printer, 1892), 42-44.

[16] "Oklahoma Territory," Oklahoma Historical Society's Encyclopedia of Oklahoma History and Culture, <http://digital.library.okstate.edu/encyclopedia/entries/O/OK085.html>, Accessed 5 April 2012.

[17] "About Guthrie Masonic Lodge #35," Guthrie Masonic Lodge #38, <http://www.guthrielodge35.org/about.php>, Accessed 5 April 2012.

[18] Grand Encampment of Knights Templar of the United States, *Proceedings of the 25th Triennial Conclave*, 42-44.

[19] John Bartlett Meserve, "The Governors of Oklahoma Territory," *The Chronicles of Oklahoma* 3 (September 1942): 222.

[20] Grand Encampment of Knights Templar of the United States, *Proceedings of the 25th Triennial Conclave*, 42-44.

[21] Creager, 172.

[22] Grand Commandery of Knights Templar of Oklahoma, *Proceedings of the 17th Annual Conclave* (Oklahoma: 1912).

[23] Most Worshipful Grand Lodge of Ancient Free and Accept Masons of Indian Territory, *Proceedings of the 16th Annual Communication* (Muskogee, I.T.: The Phoenix Steam Printing Co., 1890).

[24] Grand Commandery of Knights Templar of Indian Territory, *Proceedings of the 1st Annual*

Conclave (Indian Territory: 1895).

[25] Grand Commandery of Knights Templar of South Carolina, *Officer's Manual* (South Carolina: 1999), 6.

[26] Norman E. Angel, Kenneth S. Adams, and William A. Hensley, *History of the Grand Chapter of the Royal Arch Masons of Oklahoma* (Oklahoma: 1964), 15.

[27] Grand Encampment of Knights Templar of the United States, *Constitution, Statutes, Disciplinary Rules, Standing Resolutions, Ceremonies, Forms, and Approved Decisions* (Texas: 2011).

[28] Grand Commandery of Knights Templar of Oklahoma, *Proceedings of the 1st Annual Conclave* (Oklahoma Territory: 1896).

[29] Ibid.

[30] Ibid.

[31] Meserve, 222.

[32] Grand Commandery of Knights Templar of Oklahoma, *Proceedings of the 1st Annual Conclave*.

[33] Grand Commandery of Knights Templar of South Carolina, 6.

[34] Grand Commandery of Knights Templar of Indian Territory, *Proceedings of the 2nd Annual Conclave* (Indian Territory: 1896).

[35] Grand Commandery of Knights Templar of Oklahoma, *Proceedings of the 2nd Annual Conclave* (Oklahoma Territory: 1897).

[36] Grand Commandery of Knights Templar of Indian Territory, *Proceedings of the 2nd Annual Conclave*.

[37] Grand Commandery of Knights Templar of Indian Territory, *Proceedings of the 3rd Annual Conclave* (Indian Territory: 1897).

[38] Grand Commandery of Knights Templar of Oklahoma, *Proceedings of the 17th Annual Conclave*.

[39] Grand Commandery of Knights Templar of Oklahoma, *Proceedings of the 10th Annual Conclave* (Oklahoma Territory: 1905).

[40] Grand Commandery of Knights Templar of Oklahoma, *Proceedings of the 11th Annual Conclave* (Oklahoma Territory: 1906).

[41] Grand Commandery of Knights Templar of Indian Territory, *Proceedings of the 11th Annual Conclave* (Indian Territory: 1905).

[42] Grand Commandery of Knights Templar of Indian Territory, *Proceedings of the 12th Annual Conclave* (Indian Territory: 1906).

[43] Grand Commandery of Knights Templar of Oklahoma, *Proceedings of the 12th Annual Conclave* (Oklahoma Territory: 1907).

[44] Grand Commandery of Knights Templar of Oklahoma, *Proceedings of the 17th Annual Conclave*.

[45] Grand Commandery of Knights Templar of Indian Territory, *Proceedings of the 2nd Annual Conclave*.

[46] Grand Commandery of Knights Templar of Indian Territory, *Proceedings of the 4th Annual Conclave* (Indian Territory: 1898).

[47] Grand Commandery of Knights Templar of Indian Territory, *Proceedings of the 9th Annual Conclave* (Indian Territory: 1903).

[48] Creager, 175.

[49] Grand Commandery of Knights Templar of Indian Territory, *Proceedings of the 13th Annual Conclave* (Indian Territory: 1907).

[50] Grand Commandery of Knights Templar of Oklahoma, *Proceedings of the 9th Annual Conclave* (Oklahoma Territory: 1904).

[51] Ibid.

[52] Grand Commandery of Knights Templar of Oklahoma, *Proceedings of the 10th Annual Conclave*.

[53] Grand Commandery of Knights Templar of Indian Territory, *Proceedings of the 7th Annual Conclave* (Indian Territory: 1901).

[54] "The Snyder, Oklahoma Tornado of 10 May 1905," The National Weather Service, <http://www.srh.noaa.gov/oun/?n=events-19050510-synopsis>, Accessed 21 April 2012.

[55] Grand Commandery of Knights Templar of Oklahoma, *Proceedings of the 11th Annual Conclave*.

[56] Grand Commandery of Knights Templar of Oklahoma, *Proceedings of the 12th Annual Conclave*.

[57] Grand Commandery of Knights Templar of Indian Territory, *Proceedings of the 13th Annual Conclave* (Indian Territory: 1907).

[58] Grand Commandery of Knights Templar of Oklahoma, *Proceedings of the 16th Annual Conclave* (Oklahoma: 1911).

[59] Grand Commandery of Knights Templar of Indian Territory, *Proceedings of the 2nd Annual Conclave*.

[60] Grand Commandery of Knights Templar of Indian Territory, *Proceedings of the 8th Annual Conclave* (Indian Territory: 1902).

[61] Grand Commandery of Knights Templar of Oklahoma, *Proceedings of the 9th Annual Conclave*.

[62] Grand Commandery of Knights Templar of Oklahoma, *Proceedings of the 12th Annual Conclave*.

[63] Grand Commandery of Knights Templar of Indian Territory, *Proceedings of the 10th Annual Conclave* (Indian Territory: 1904).

[64] Grand Commandery of Knights Templar of Indian Territory, *Proceedings of the 12th Annual Conclave*.

[65] Grand Commandery of Knights Templar of Oklahoma, *Proceedings of the 16th Annual Conclave*.

[66] Grand Commandery of Knights Templar of Indian Territory, *Proceedings of the 8th Annual Conclave*.

[67] Grand Commandery of Knights Templar of Indian Territory, *Proceedings of the 13th Annual Conclave*.

[68] Grand Commandery of Knights Templar of Oklahoma, *Proceedings of the 8th Annual Conclave* (Oklahoma Territory: 1903).

[69] Grand Commandery of Knights Templar of Oklahoma, *Proceedings of the 7th Annual Conclave* (Oklahoma Territory: 1902).

[70] "Former Dean Profile: Edwin C. DeBarr," The University of Oklahoma College of Pharmacy, <http://pharmacy.ouhsc.edu/about/history/deans/debarr.asp>, Accessed 21 April 2012.

[71] Creager, 182.

[72] Grand Commandery of Knights Templar of Indian Territory, *Proceedings of the 3rd Annual Conclave*.

[73] Grand Commandery of Knights Templar of Indian Territory, *Proceedings of the 6th Annual Conclave* (Indian Territory: 1900).

[74] Grand Commandery of Knights Templar of Oklahoma, *Proceedings of the 7th Annual Conclave* (Oklahoma Territory: 1902).

[75] Grand Commandery of Knights Templar of Oklahoma, *Proceedings of the 13th Annual Conclave* (Oklahoma: 1908).

[76] Grand Commandery of Knights Templar of Indian Territory, *Proceedings of the 5th Annual Conclave* (Indian Territory: 1899).

[77] Grand Commandery of Knights Templar of Oklahoma, *Proceedings of the 15th Annual Conclave* (Oklahoma: 1910).

[78] Grand Commandery of Knights Templar of Indian Territory, *Proceedings of the 5th Annual Conclave*.

[79] Grand Commandery of Knights Templar of Oklahoma, *Proceedings of the 13th Annual Conclave* (Oklahoma: 1908).

[80] Grand Commandery of Knights Templar of Oklahoma, *Proceedings of the 11th Annual Conclave*.

[81] Grand Commandery of Knights Templar of Indian Territory, *Proceedings of the 11th Annual Conclave* (Indian Territory: 1905).

[82] Grand Commandery of Knights Templar of Indian Territory, *Proceedings of the 12th Annual Conclave*.

[83] "Statehood Movement," Oklahoma Historical Society's Encyclopedia of Oklahoma History and Culture, <http://digital.library.okstate.edu/encyclopedia/entries/S/ST025.html>, Accessed 2 July 2012.

[84] Creager, 181-182.

[85] Grand Commandery of Knights Templar of Indian Territory, *Proceedings of the 14th Annual Conclave* (Oklahoma: 1908).

[86] Grand Commandery of Knights Templar of Oklahoma, *Proceedings of the 16th Annual Conclave*.

[87] Creager, 182-183.

[88] Ibid, 185.

[89] Grand Commandery of Knights Templar of Oklahoma, *Special Conclave for the Purpose of Consolidation* (Oklahoma: 1911).

[90] Creager, 185.

[91] Grand Commandery of Knights Templar of Oklahoma, *Special Conclave for the Purpose of Consolidation*.

Images from the Oklahoma Historical Society

Pawnee Commandery No. 7, 20699.2009.182.2024.2.B, Currie Ballard Collection, OHS Research Division.

II: Prosperity Abounds

For the world, the next nineteen years would yield opportunities to rejoice and opportunities to mourn. The maiden voyage of the *RMS Titanic* would end in tragedy in the spring of 1912. The First World War would commence in 1914 and consume the lives of some nine million people. A period of great economic prosperity would abound during the 1920s, but it would come crashing down in 1929. The Sir Knights of Oklahoma would experience the same woes as the rest of the world, but in true Templar fashion they carried on in the face of adversity.

With consolidation now complete, the first order of business for the Grand Commandery of Oklahoma was bringing two sets of constituent Commanderies in line as one. The Constitution of the Grand Encampment of Knights Templar of the United States requires Commanderies to be numbered according to date of their charter, which made the renumbering fairly easy with the exception of the first three Commanderies of the old jurisdictions. This was due to the original three Commanderies of each jurisdiction being chartered by the Grand Encampment. To resolve the issue, Guthrie, Muskogee, Oklahoma, Ascension, Chickasaw, and McAlester Commanderies were all numbered according to the date of their dispensation to work. As such, these six Commanderies were renumbered as follows: Guthrie No. 1, Muskogee No. 2, Oklahoma No. 3, Ascension No. 4, Chickasaw No. 5, and McAlester No. 6.[1] The year 1912 would also see the establishment of two new Commanderies. Both Shawnee No. 36 and St. Augustine No. 37 at Alva were issued charters on April 19, 1912.[2]

While the presence of so called "sojourning" Sir Knights was becoming less common, the panhandle of Oklahoma was still in many aspects a frontier. It was noted in 1913 that while there were forty Royal Arch Masons belonging to the Chapter in Guymon, only three of them had pursued the Orders of Templary. The main reason for this lack of "advancement" was due to the nearest Oklahoma Commandery being 165 miles away in Taloga. To settle what was known as "The Guymon Matter," the Grand Commandery of Oklahoma gave the Masons residing there two options: petition for the Templar Orders in Oklahoma with courtesy work being performed in Kansas (courtesy work is the conferral of degrees upon a candidate by one jurisdiction at the request of another) or petition for the Templar Orders in Oklahoma with work being performed in Oklahoma. Apparently neither of these options was attractive to the Masons of Guymon and they petitioned for membership with Liberal Commandery No. 55 at Liberal, Kansas, which was only 40 miles away. Grand Commander Guy Bohannon of course objected to this, but in time gave his consent as Guymon was so far removed from the rest of the Commanderies in Oklahoma.[3] Ultimately "Concurrent Jurisdiction" would be established with Liberal, Kansas, for the Sir Knights in Guymon allowing them to freely petition for membership in the Commandery there. Similar courtesies were established with Dalhart, Texas, in 1923 for Masons living in Boise City.[4]

In the years that passed from 1914 to 1927, a total of twelve Commanderies would be established. It was certainly an era of prosperity and this can easily be seen in the annual reports of the Grand Recorder. In 1914 there was a total of 2,378 Sir Knights in Oklahoma.[5] By 1925 the ranks had swollen to 7,425.[6] Amidst all this chartering it was noted in 1916 that the Grand Commandery of Oklahoma had never received a physical charter itself from the Grand Encampment.[7] After a considerable amount of correspondence with the Grand Encampment, Most Excellent Grand Master George W. Vallery issued a charter to Oklahoma in 1926.[8] One town that expressed an interest in a Commandery was Woodward. They received the blessing of the Sir Knights of St. Aumer at Taloga in 1917, but Grand Commander James Louthan had something different in mind. It had been noted that St. Aumer had been dormant and rather than taking steps to arrest their charter, they were encouraged to move to Woodward.[9]

Unfortunately not every Commandery had the luxury of another town with a desire for a Commandery nearby. In 1920, Foraker No. 34 would lose their charter due to inactivity.[10] Sir Knights residing in Altus secured a dispensation to work in 1924 but it was revoked in 1927 as interest waned.[11] A similar situation arose in Cheyenne who had secured a dispensation to work in 1921 only to lose it the following year.[12] The Sir Knights of Durant No. 31 suffered a fate similar to Foraker No. 34 in 1928. Grand Commander Bert Ashbrook was forced to seize Durant's charter after a two year lapse in per capita tax payment to the Grand Commandery.[13]

The drums of war were beginning to sound in Europe in 1914 and the Sir Knights of Oklahoma could hear their call. In his address to the Sir Knights, Grand Commander Angus Gillis spoke of peace almost as if he was hoping the world would hear his plea. His remarks were certainly made to strike accord with the Christian Knights he was addressing:

> In connection with the thought of death, our minds naturally turn to the death and devastation that is being waged by war in the old world. There is no civilized warfare, and when I was elected Grand Commander I had in mind many things to say about the barbarity of war but the European conflict now raging has so exaggerated all forms of destruction that the horrors and distress, the suffering and humiliation caused by the greed for power with no thought or care for the ruin and loss that it causes or the backward sweep that it gives civilization, is beyond my imagined and powers of expression.
>
> Think of the enormous expenditures made in preparation for war; think of the loss of lives, the destruction of property – and to what end. It ruins homes and prosperity, it destroys hopes and ambitions, it blasts all that is good and elevating and leaves as assets and accomplishments only the maimed, the crippled, and the vicious, together with innocent maidens, destitute widows, helpless orphans, and a total disregard for the Christian religion.[14]

Gillis was a medical doctor by profession and would serve in the Medical Corps of the US Army during The Great War. He was

Grand Commandery assembled at Oklahoma City in 1914

Courtesy of the Grand Commandery of Oklahoma

not the only Sir Knight to answer the call, when the Grand Commandery convened in 1917 it was noted that a number of the Grand Officers were in the service of their country. In what can only be described as an act of respect for their sacrifice, the absent officers were advanced to their next offices accordingly.[15] Of course, the constituent Commanderies also saw members leave their Asylums for service in Europe. In 1918 Gethsemane No. 25 elected their Eminent Commander while he was away with the military.[16] The Great War, as it was then called, brought levels of carnage to humanity that had never before been seen. Described as the first modern war, World War One saw a number of advancements in the art of destruction including machine guns, tanks, and chemical weapons. In his 1918 address, Grand Commander Eugene McMahan painted a vivid picture for the Sir Knights of the killing that had consumed Europe:

> It was our hope that the forces of right would prevail speedily, and that the children of men might again dwell together in peace; but such has not been permitted, and at this present hour nearly the whole European continent is engaged in human butchery and sweltering in human blood.[17]

Peace would finally settle like the autumn leaves at the eleventh hour, on the eleventh day, of the eleventh month in 1918.

The Selective Service Act of 1917 saw some 2.8 million men drafted into military service, but those who were either too old or unable to serve stayed behind.[18] The Sir Knights who remained in the United States took up the war effort at home. When war broke out in Europe there were of course Americans traveling abroad and some of them happened to be Templars. To aide these stranded Sir Knights, a war relief emergency fund was created by the Grand Encampment with each Sir Knight nationwide contributing $1.[19] The brainchild of Past Grand Master William B. Melish, this fund would expand into the Masonic War Relief Association and collect $140,011 for the relief of Masonic widows and orphans in Europe. While expending some $150,000 themselves on foreign orphans, Knights Templar across the United States would contribute $20,783 to Melish's fund.[20] The Grand Encampment's relief for orphans was provided through the Fatherless Children of France organization, by which one hundred French orphans were "adopted." This was done at a cost of $73 each with the membership of the Grand Encampment, current and Past Grand Commanders, paying the sum.[21] Naturally these men could turn to the Sir Knights of their respective Grand Jurisdictions and not only meet the required amount but exceed it.

War relief was not the only manner in which the Sir Knights of Oklahoma helped with the war effort. The entire country was being urged to invest in Liberty Bonds and by 1919 the Grand Commandery held $3,000 in such bonds.[22] The Sir Knights of Oklahoma not only invested in Liberty Bonds, they also took an active role in helping to sell them. It can easily be said that parading was an essential part of fraternalism in the early twentieth century and patriotic parades were abundant during World War I. Ardmore No. 9 and Ada No. 16 both appeared in Liberty Bond parades. The Sir Knights of Elk City No. 22 appeared in uniform with the American Red Cross and Poteau No. 40 participated in a War Savings Stamp Book drive. The Sir Knights also made sacrifices of their own. Perhaps the most appealing part of Templary to the candidate is the Sir Knight resplendent in his full dress uniform. Originally when a man petitioned for membership in his local Commandery, a fee was collected to purchase his uniform. Due to shortages during the war, this requirement of the uniform fee was suspended as uniforms could not easily be had.[23]

The tactics and precision movements executed by Knights Templar on parade no doubt served those Sir Knights who entered military service well. It had become the tradition for the annual conclave of the Grand Commandery to commence with a parade. A description of the 1924 parade in Oklahoma City provides a glimpse of what the spectators observed that day:

> With the first note of the trumpet, mounted aides broke from the side of the Grand Marshal, sharp commands came from the division commanders, the long line of plumed knights stiffened, swords flashed in the brilliant rays of the morning sun, and one of the most elaborate pageants ever witnessed by Oklahoma City was sweeping down Broadway, the colors of this ancient and magnanimous order fluttering in the breeze, and nearly one thousand

Frederick Commandery No. 19 Asylum Drill Team in 1914
Courtesy of the Grand Commandery of Oklahoma

Enid Commandery No. 13 Asylum Drill Team in 1917
Courtesy of the Grand Commandery of Oklahoma

Knights of the Cross and Crown, with the waving of snowy white plumes against glossy black of their uniforms, thrilled thousands of spectators massed along the line of march.[24]

The war years and immediately after saw the establishment of both Asylum and Field Drill competitions. The first Asylum Drill competition was held in 1916.[25] An Asylum Drill is simply the tactics for opening a Commandery of Knights Templar and Commanderies were being graded on this through the annual inspection process prior to the establishment of the competition. Grand Commander Angus Gillis found several advantages in the inspection process, those being enthusiasm among Commanderies and it allowed the Grand Commander to become acquainted with each Commandery. The only flaw Gillis observed was that no one Inspector could inspect all of the Commanderies and this led to differences in grades.[26] To remedy this, the Commanderies were to compete in opening a Commandery at the annual conclave of the Grand Commandery. While there was only one entry, Frederick No. 19, the first competition was a success.[27]

In the early days of the Grand Commandery, the annual conclave was mostly a private affair for the Sir Knights and their Ladies. In time, the parades that marked the opening of the conclave grew in size and began to draw the attention of the general public. When the Field Drill competition was officially added in 1921, the public turned out to enjoy the spectacle.[28] Grand Commander Gillis had a desire to promote drill activities as early as 1915 when he issued General Order No. 2. He felt that seeing Templars in uniform created a desire in many Royal Arch Masons to receive the "pleasures and benefits of Templar membership."[29] It is likely that many of the returning servicemen who took the Degrees of Freemasonry found the activities of the Knights Templar interesting and viewed them as something they could relate to. In order to accommodate all of the Commanderies of Oklahoma, two days for drill competition were setup outside of the annual conclave of the Grand Commandery. Competitions were to be held one day in Eastern Oklahoma and a separate day in Western Oklahoma.[30] A Templar drill team in motion is certainly a sight to see as they execute intricate movements such as forming the cross and those who filled the grandstands were duly entertained. Grand Commander elect

Oklahoma Commandery No. 3 Field Drill Team

Trinity Commandery No. 20 Field Drill Team

Bethlehem Commandery No. 45 Field Drill Team

Ben Hur Commandery No. 14 Field Drill Team
All courtesy of the Grand Commandery of Oklahoma

Ascension Commandery No. 4 Field Drill Team

Cushing Commandery No. 42 Field Drill Team

Muskogee Commandery No. 2 Field Drill Team
All courtesy of the Grand Commandery of Oklahoma

Field Drill Competitions in 1922
Courtesy of the Grand Commandery of Oklahoma

Grand Parade in 1922

Courtesy of the Grand Commandery of Oklahoma

Grand Commandery "Color Band" in 1925
Courtesy of the Grand Commandery of Oklahoma

Parade Marshal's Mounted Aides in 1925
Courtesy of the Grand Commandery of Oklahoma

Reviewing Stand at Grand Parade in 1925
Courtesy of the Grand Commandery of Oklahoma

Harold Downing was most pleased with the first drill competition and hoped that more teams would be fielded in the coming years in addition to the three that competed in 1921; those being Oklahoma No. 3, Enid No. 13, and Trinity No. 20. At the urging of Downing, drill badges similar to those of Kansas were adopted and awarded to those Sir Knights who participated in the competition.[31]

The Twenties were a period of great growth for Freemasonry in general. The war saw many servicemen taking the Degrees and many of them also pursued the "higher" Degrees. One Scottish Rite Reunion in Guthrie witnessed over two hundred servicemen come up from Camp Doniphan at Fort Sill. To meet the needs of the military men, a Masonic "club house" was erected at Fort Sill for the purpose of communicating the Degrees of the Scottish Rite on soldiers.[32] The Knights Templar in Oklahoma also saw a swell in membership with it reaching its height in 1925 with 7,425 Sir Knights.[33] With all these men joining the ranks of the Fraternity, massive building projects were undertaken to accommodate the Brethren. It was noted in 1923 that $5 to $6 million was being spent on Masonic construction in the State.[34] The Masons of Oklahoma City began construction of a new Masonic Temple to be located at the corner of Northwest Sixth and Robinson. A Masonic Temple Building Association was formed in order to finance the building with a number of Masonic bodies joining together, of these Oklahoma No. 3 and Bethlehem No. 45 were included. The new Oklahoma City Temple was completed in 1923 at a cost of over $1 million and though no longer functioning as a Masonic hall, the building still stands today. Housed inside was a Shrine auditorium capable of seating 3,000 people, a smaller auditorium dubbed Harding Hall that could seat 700, assorted social rooms including a billiards room, and a ballroom.[35] The building also held five lodge rooms and two York Rite (the collective term for Royal Arch Masons, Cryptic Masons, and Knights Templar) specific meeting halls.[36]

Just up the road from Oklahoma City, the Scottish Rite Masons of Guthrie were commencing a monumental construction project. While the State Capitol had moved to Oklahoma City, the old Capitol Hill and meeting hall remained in Guthrie. After the designs for a Methodist University on the grounds fell through,

The Oklahoma City Masonic Temple at Northwest Sixth and Robinson

Courtesy of the Oklahoma Historical Society

Commandery Asylum of the Oklahoma City Masonic Temple
Courtesy of the Oklahoma Historical Society

the Guthrie Scottish Rite was able to secure the land for the grand sum of one dollar.[37] The ground breaking for the new Temple in Guthrie occurred on May 6, 1920, and a few months later the cornerstone for the Temple was laid. The cornerstone ceremony was preceded by a grand parade in which numerous Masonic groups marched; one of those being the Sir Knights of Guthrie No. 1. It was noted that some 8,000 spectators were on hand for the ceremony on January 20, 1921. The new Scottish Rite Temple was completed in 1924 and was dubbed the largest Masonic structure in the world.[38] The Scottish Rite Brethren of McAlester also began an expansion project of their own in 1928 to accommodate their growing membership of 6,000. From the bowels of their existing Temple completed in 1907, the largest stage in the Southern Jurisdiction of the Ancient & Accepted Scottish Rite was carved.[39] McAlester was of course no stranger to Masonic edifices; McAlester Commandery No. 6 had the luxury of their own meeting hall while the Royal Arch Masons and Council of Royal and Select Masters met in what can only be described as an awe inspiring temple north of town known as Mount Moriah.[40]

    Masonic meeting halls were not the only structures going up courtesy of Masonic treasuries. Again the Masons of McAlester where at the helm though the structure was by no means in McAlester. In 1919 the McAlester Scottish Rite earmarked $100,000 to construct a Masonic dormitory on the campus of the University of Oklahoma. Located at the corner of Boyd and University, a portion of the building was also home to the Acacia social fraternity; their membership was originally limited to Master Masons.[41] By 1920, the Grand Lodge of Oklahoma was looking to separate and relocate the children and elderly who comprised the Masonic Home at Darlington. There was a general belief that the children would have better opportunities to learn a trade and obtain employment if closer to a metro area as Darlington was, and still is, relatively isolated. A location for what would become the Masonic Children's Home was found in Guthrie in 1922 and Leslie Swan, who would go on to serve as Grand Commander, laid the cornerstone in 1923.[42] For a period, no great municipal building in the State was complete unless it bore a Masonic cornerstone. When the Grand

Laying the Cornerstone of the Bryan County Courthouse on July 4, 1917

Courtesy of the Oklahoma Historical Society

Lodge of Oklahoma assembled to lay the cornerstone of the new State Capitol at Oklahoma City on November 16, 1915, the Sir Knights of Oklahoma No. 3 were present to serve as escort to the Grand Master.[43] While many cornerstone ceremonies would be held through the years, that particular one is undoubtedly the most important and a shining moment for Freemasonry in Oklahoma.

During his tenure as Grand Commander, Angus Gillis instituted a great many programs for the Sir Knights. It is evident that his vision was to enhance the Order and secure its future, which he played a major role in. The Commanderies had previously been grouped into districts for administrative purposes so that Grand Officers could be assigned to visit specific Commanderies and see that all was operating accordingly. Gillis took this idea further and in 1915 he organized the Grand Commandery into "Triangles" to provide for joint conclaves amongst the Commanderies.[44] This was a move to promote camaraderie among Commanderies and give smaller Commanderies an opportunity to participate in Templar activities their limited membership may have prevented them from doing. A by product of these joint conclaves was also recruitment for new Sir Knights. Gillis was of the opinion that solicitation for membership must commence immediately following the Entered Apprentice Degree of Ancient Craft Masonry. He wanted to "crown their Masonic studies with the knowledge of the capstone of American Masonry, the Commandery Orders."[45]

The First World War of course provided ample opportunities for charitable giving by the Sir Knights of Oklahoma, but war did not generate the only need by those less fortunate. Charitable giving to the Masonic Boys Home, which would ultimately move to Guthrie, was maintained throughout the period that led up to 1929.[46] When hostilities ceased in 1918, the Grand Encampment's War Relief Fund was transformed into the Educational Loan Fund.[47] When Most Excellent Grand Master Leonidas P. Newby established the fund, he said "let us make more thinkers or let us help more folks to straight thinking."[48] By 1928 the fund had loaned $30,375 to students, male and female, in Oklahoma alone.[49] The maximum amount a student could borrow a year with the fund was $200, which in today's money would be roughly $2,600.[50] The Roaring Twenties also brought devastating storms to the Nation and Oklahoma answered the call. The "Great Miami Hurricane" of 1926 made landfall as a category 4 storm and damaged or destroyed every building in the downtown district of Miami.[51] The following year the most destructive floods in the history of the United States struck the Mississippi River Valley. To provide relief for those affected, $600 was dispatched for both disasters.[52] Of course, those who call Oklahoma home are no strangers to storms themselves. It was in the spring of 1928 that one of those great storms appeared on the horizon in Shawnee, Oklahoma. The tornado that dropped from the skies on April 4th even lifted a two story home from its foundation and placed it neatly across the railroad tracks.[53] The Grand Commandery was able to send $100 to Shawnee in the wake of the storm.[54]

As a Christian Order, there are two major events in the year for Knights Templar; Christmas and Easter. The Grand Encampment of Knights Templar of the United States required the Sir Knights of its jurisdiction to observe these two holidays officially. For Easter this would entail the Sir Knights assembling in their Asylum on Easter Sunday and proceeding to a church of their choice for service. In his General Order calling for the Easter Observance in 1917, Grand Commander James Louthan stated:

> Let the ceremonies of this occasion be such that the Word may be spoken faithfully, the faith kept securely and the secure doctrine of Templar Masonry truly promulgated. Let there be the assuring lesson of patience and perseverance for the weary pilgrim; and, for the child of humility, the comforting hope of a risen Christ.[55]

In 1923 the Sir Knights of Oklahoma No. 3 and Bethlehem No. 45 held a joint Easter Observance in which four hundred Sir Knights were in attendance.[56] The annual Christmas Observance also called for the Sir Knights to assemble in their Asylum and was no less grand of an occasion than the Easter Observance.[57]

The Sir Knights certainly made excellent showings at their assorted activities throughout the years and the Triennial Conclave of the Grand Encampment was no exception. The 35th Triennial at New Orleans in 1922 saw close to 12,000 Sir Knights march in

Combined Easter Service of Oklahoma No. 3 and Bethlehem No. 45 in 1922

Courtesy of the Grand Commandery of Oklahoma

Sir Knights from Oklahoma at New Orleans for the 35th Triennial in 1922

Courtesy of the Grand Commandery of Oklahoma

the grand parade. Oklahoma had been encouraged to attend in mass as the state had been part of the Louisiana Purchase and while an Oklahoman today may not feel a "connection" with Louisiana, 135 Sir Knights and a handful of their Ladies made the trek to New Orleans.[58] It was at the 35th Triennial that Charles Tedrowe began to gain the attention of the powers that be at the national level of Templary. Tedrowe would serve as Grand Commander of Oklahoma in 1925 and that same year he visited the Grand Commandery of Kansas as the personal representative of Most Excellent Grand Master Leonidas P. Newby.[59] That summer Charles Tedrowe would be appointed Grand Warder of the Grand Encampment while in session at Seattle.[60] While relatively young, the Sir Knights of Oklahoma had truly arrived by securing their first officer of the Grand Encampment. Tedrowe held the office of Grand Warder through two Triennials and it was believed by the Sir Knights of Oklahoma that he would ultimately become Grand Master of the Order. After active campaigning for Tedrowe to be elected Grand Junior Warden in 1931, he lost the bid but maintained a committee presence with the Grand Encampment for a number of years.[61]

When the Order of DeMolay for boys was founded in 1919, it quickly found a friend in the Knights Templar. The fact that the youth group took its name from the last Grand Master of the ancient Knights Templar certainly helped foster this relationship.[62] Grand Commander Harold Downing took up the banner in 1922 and strongly encouraged his constituent Commanderies to sponsor chapters of DeMolay in their respective cities.[63] As the youth group spread across Oklahoma the Sir Knights made sure boys everywhere wanted to join. Muskogee No. 2, Calvary No. 26, and Claremore No. 41 all marched in parades for the institution of new chapters of DeMolay in their respective cities.[64]

In 1928 the Sir Knights of Miami Commandery No. 49 organized an event of truly "grand" proportions. On February 16th a "Four State Conclave" was held with Sir Knights from Kansas, Missouri, Arkansas, and Oklahoma in attendance. Those Sir Knights who made the trek to Miami that day enjoyed drill exhibitions and a conferral of the Order of the Temple.[65] It was a fitting close to a decade of incredible success for the Sir Knights of Oklahoma and Freemasonry as a whole. Little did they know, or anyone for that matter, that on October 24, 1929, the prosperity that had endured would be forever changed.

Officers of the Grand Commandery and Past Grand Commanders of Oklahoma in 1927

Courtesy of the Grand Commandery of Oklahoma

Notes

[1] Grand Commandery of Knights Templar of Oklahoma, *Proceedings of the 17th Annual Conclave* (Oklahoma: 1912).

[2] Grand Commandery of Knights Templar of Oklahoma, *Proceedings of the 18th Annual Conclave* (Oklahoma: 1913).

[3] Ibid.

[4] Grand Commandery of Knights Templar of Oklahoma, *Proceedings of the 28th Annual Conclave* (Oklahoma: 1923).

[5] Grand Commandery of Knights Templar of Oklahoma, *Proceedings of the 19th Annual Conclave* (Oklahoma: 1914).

[6] Grand Commandery of Knights Templar of Oklahoma, *Proceedings of the 30th Annual Conclave* (Oklahoma: 1925).

[7] Grand Commandery of Knights Templar of Oklahoma, *Proceedings of the 21st Annual Conclave* (Oklahoma: 1916).

[8] Grand Commandery of Knights Templar of Oklahoma, *Proceedings of the 32nd Annual Conclave* (Oklahoma: 1927).

[9] Grand Commandery of Knights Templar of Oklahoma, *Proceedings of the 22nd Annual Conclave* (Oklahoma: 1917).

[10] Grand Commandery of Knights Templar of Oklahoma, *Proceedings of the 25th Annual Conclave* (Oklahoma: 1920).

[11] Grand Commandery of Knights Templar of Oklahoma, *Proceedings of the 32nd Annual Conclave*.

[12] Grand Commandery of Knights Templar of Oklahoma, *Proceedings of the 27th Annual Conclave* (Oklahoma: 1922).

[13] Grand Commandery of Knights Templar of Oklahoma, *Proceedings of the 33rd Annual Conclave* (Oklahoma: 1928).

[14] Grand Commandery of Knights Templar of Oklahoma, *Proceedings of the 20th Annual Conclave* (Oklahoma: 1915).

[15] Charles E. Creager, *History of Freemasonry in Oklahoma* (Muskogee, Oklahoma: Muskogee Print Shop, 1935), 187-189.

[16] Grand Commandery of Knights Templar of Oklahoma, *Proceedings of the 23rd Annual Conclave* (Oklahoma: 1918).

[17] Ibid.

[18] "History and Records," Selective Service System, <http://www.sss.gov/induct.htm>, Accessed 6 June 2012.

[19] Grand Commandery of Knights Templar of Oklahoma, *Proceedings of the 23rd Annual Conclave*.

[20] "Masonic War Relief Association," Mackey's Encyclopedia of Freemasonry, <http://www.freemason.com/library/macenc35.htm>, Accessed 6 June 2012.

[21] Grand Commandery of Knights Templar of Oklahoma, *Proceedings of the 24th Annual Conclave* (Oklahoma: 1919).

[22] Ibid.

[23] Grand Commandery of Knights Templar of Oklahoma, *Proceedings of the 29th Annual Conclave* (Oklahoma: 1924).

[24] Ibid.

[25] Grand Commandery of Knights Templar of Oklahoma, *Proceedings of the 21st Annual Conclave*.

[26] Grand Commandery of Knights Templar of Oklahoma, *Proceedings of the 20th Annual Conclave.*

[27] Grand Commandery of Knights Templar of Oklahoma, *Proceedings of the 21st Annual Conclave.*

[28] Grand Commandery of Knights Templar of Oklahoma, *Proceedings of the 26th Annual Conclave* (Oklahoma: 1921).

[29] Grand Commandery of Knights Templar of Oklahoma, *Proceedings of the 20th Annual Conclave.*

[30] Grand Commandery of Knights Templar of Oklahoma, *Proceedings of the 26th Annual Conclave* (Oklahoma: 1921).

[31] Ibid.

[32] *The Oklahoma Consistory* (January 1918), Vol. 3, No. 1.

[33] Grand Commandery of Knights Templar of Oklahoma, *Proceedings of the 30th Annual Conclave.*

[34] Grand Commandery of Knights Templar of Oklahoma, *Proceedings of the 28th Annual Conclave.*

[35] Gene McKelvey, *The Masonic History of the Murrah Building Bombing Memorial Museum* (Oklahoma: The Oklahoma Lodge of Research), 1-4.

[36] Grand Commandery of Knights Templar of Oklahoma, *Proceedings of the 28th Annual Conclave.*

[37] Robert G. Davis and Frank A. Derr, *100 Years of Scottish Rite Masonry in the Valley of Guthrie* (Oklahoma: Guthrie Valley AASR), 80-91.

[38] Ibid, 96-134.

[39] "History of the Center," McAlester Scottish Rite Masonic Center, <http://www.mcalesterscottishrite.org/HistoryMSR.htm>, Accessed 7 June 2012.

[40] Charles E. Creager, "The Crypt at McAlester, Oklahoma," The Phoenixmasonry Masonic Museum and Library, <http://www.phoenixmasonry.org/the_builder_1919_july.htm>, Accessed 7 June 2012.

[41] Davis and Derr, 99-100.

[42] Ibid, 99-123.

[43] Grand Commandery of Knights Templar of Oklahoma, *Proceedings of the 21st Annual Conclave.*

[44] Grand Commandery of Knights Templar of Oklahoma, *Proceedings of the 20th Annual Conclave.*

[45] Ibid.

[46] Grand Commandery of Knights Templar of Oklahoma, *Proceedings of the 18th Annual Conclave.*

[47] Creager, *History of Freemasonry in Oklahoma*, 188.

[48] Grand Commandery of Knights Templar of Oklahoma, *Proceedings of the 28th Annual Conclave.*

[49] Grand Commandery of Knights Templar of Oklahoma, *Proceedings of the 33rd Annual Conclave.*

[50] Grand Commandery of Knights Templar of Oklahoma, *Proceedings of the 28th Annual Conclave.*

[51] "Hurricanes in History," National Oceanic and Atmospheric Administration, <http://www.nhc.noaa.gov/outreach/history/#miami26>, Accessed 10 June 2012.

[52] Grand Commandery of Knights Templar of Oklahoma, *Proceedings of the 32nd Annual Conclave.*

[53] "Pottawatomie County Postcards," Rootsweb, <http://www.rootsweb.ancestry.com/~okpcgc/postcards/postcard_album.html>, Accessed 10 June 2012.

[54] Grand Commandery of Knights Templar of Oklahoma, *Proceedings of the 33rd Annual Conclave*.

[55] Grand Commandery of Knights Templar of Oklahoma, *Proceedings of the 22nd Annual Conclave*.

[56] Grand Commandery of Knights Templar of Oklahoma, *Proceedings of the 28th Annual Conclave*.

[57] Grand Commandery of Knights Templar of Oklahoma, *Proceedings of the 22nd Annual Conclave*.

[58] Grand Commandery of Knights Templar of Oklahoma, *Proceedings of the 27th Annual Conclave*.

[59] Grand Commandery of Knights Templar of Oklahoma, *Proceedings of the 30th Annual Conclave*.

[60] Grand Commandery of Knights Templar of Oklahoma, *Proceedings of the 31st Annual Conclave* (Oklahoma: 1926).

[61] Grand Commandery of Knights Templar of Oklahoma, *Proceedings of the 36th Annual Conclave* (Oklahoma: 1931).

[62] "History of DeMolay," DeMolay International, <http://www.demolay.org/aboutdemolay/history.php>, Accessed 10 June 2012.

[63] Grand Commandery of Knights Templar of Oklahoma, *Proceedings of the 27th Annual Conclave*.

[64] Ibid.

[65] Grand Commandery of Knights Templar of Oklahoma, *Proceedings of the 33rd Annual Conclave*.

Images from the Oklahoma Historical Society

Oklahoma City Masonic Temple, 22697.21, George Forsyth Collection, OHS Research Division.

Commandery Asylum, 21412.M21.1, Barney Hillerman Collection, OHS Research Division.

Bryan County Courthouse Cornerstone Laying, 21356, Oklahoma Historical Society Oversize Photograph Collection, OHS Research Division.

III: Dark Days

The 1930s saw the most devastating economic down turn in history take hold across the world. The unemployment rate in the United States would rise to 25%, while some countries saw a rate as high as 33%.[1] As farmers were facing ruin in the wake of falling prices, those of the Great Plains, and more specifically Oklahoma, were dealt an even heavier blow as "The Dust Bowl" set in. The years 1934 and 1936 would yield intense droughts coupled with poor soil conversation that resulted in massive dust storms sweeping across the land.[2] Some who called Oklahoma home found themselves leaving the state just to survive. The 1930s also saw hostilities flair in Europe again. Freemasonry as a whole was not immune to the problems that were wreaking havoc on the world, but the institution and the Sir Knights who supported it stood resolute.

The men that comprised Templary in Oklahoma entered the Great Depression in a position of strength. Their numbers were soaring and the finances relatively secure; investments and cash in the treasury in 1930 totaled $30,520. The loss of membership to the Order nationwide was already being experienced though. Most Excellent Grand Master William L. Sharp of the Grand Encampment was present at the 35th Annual Conclave of Oklahoma and remarked that the present losses were mostly due to suspensions of members in Blue Lodges and Chapters of Royal Arch Masons.[3] There was a movement to end the requirement of continued affiliation with Royal Arch Masonry once a man became a Knight Templar, the idea being that two sovereign orders should be able to stand on their own. Fortunately for Royal Arch Masonry, there was no wide spread support for this idea in Templary.[4] By 1931 numbers in

Grand Commandery assembled at Muskogee in 1930
Courtesy of the Grand Commandery of Oklahoma

Oklahoma were declining, and fairly drastically. The Report of the Grand Recorder shows 6,569 Sir Knights in Oklahoma and Grand Commander Ralph V. Downing noted this in his address:

> The membership in this Grand Jurisdiction has shown a slightly larger decrease than last year. That this should be true in a year of distressing economic conditions following a year of unprecedented prosperity is not surprising.[5]

By 1932 the membership had decreased even further to 6,127 Sir Knights. In an effort to curb further losses, James A. Lathim proposed the remission of dues for indigent and sick Sir Knights with their home Commanderies not being required to pay the per capita tax on their membership to the Grand Commandery.[6] While the idea was noble, such a measure would have further crippled the Grand Commandery financially and was not adopted.

The inspection reports of 1931 show that a number of Commanderies were found to be in "unsatisfactory condition."[7] With the Depression in its early days, the time was at hand to begin shoring up the foundation of the Order in Oklahoma. By 1934, three Commanderies had surrendered their charters and the Sir Knights of Chickasaw No. 5 in Purcell were fortunate enough to consolidate with Norman No. 38.[8] The general fund, cash on hand, in 1934 had decreased to $2,746; down from $10,660 in 1924. The Grand Recorder noted that this sum was insufficient to cover the operating costs of the Grand Commandery.[9] With only 4,084 Sir Knights in 1936, the Grand Recorder made sure to champion his now "lean" operating expenses.[10] By 1937, it was not just individual Sir Knights who had become unable to pay their dues. The Commanderies at Perry, Frederick, and Eldorado were all delinquent in their per capita tax payments to the Grand Commandery that year.[11] While it would be many years before another Commandery was chartered in Oklahoma, Grand Commander John I. Taylor was a man of action and did his very best to ensure the survival of the Order. It was during his tenure in 1940 that three Commanderies were consolidated with others nearby and an additional four charters were returned to the Grand Commandery.[12]

Any Masonic body's financial survival is dependent upon a membership that is able to pay its dues, as that is the primary source of revenue. With a membership struggling to make ends meet, it was only a matter of time before the Masonic Bodies dependent upon their dues began to struggle and lose assets. The 1920s saw a great many Masonic construction projects, most of which were still being paid for when the market crashed in 1929. The Scottish Rite Masons of McAlester had installed a magnificent organ in their third Temple. The 3,100 pipe organ had been ordered from the Kimball Company in 1929 and was housed in the ceiling of the auditorium. Shortly there after, it was clear that the Masonic leadership in McAlester would be unable to make payments for the organ and representatives from Kimball came to repossess it. Upon their arrival, the Kimball men found the organ situated at the top of a four-story spiral staircase and quickly agreed to work with the McAlester Scottish Rite on payments.[13] The Sir Knights of Oklahoma City who had joined with other Masonic groups to construct a Temple at 621 N. Broadway found themselves in a situation much worse than late payments for a pipe organ. The majority of the Temple in Oklahoma City had been financed by India Shrine and as their membership began to decrease they looked for means to save the Temple. After attempts to rent commercial space in the Temple, the property was ultimately turned back over to the lender in 1931.[14] While "depression" was everywhere, Grand Commander Walter M. Rainey delivered a message of hope in 1934:

> The depression has taken its toll; conditions have been disturbed, but, I have no fear for Templarism. I believe that Templarism is just as fundmentally sound today, as it was in the days of Richard the Lionhearted…
>
> … we have had some losses, but I believe the brilliant rays of the rising sun will dispel the dark and gloomy clouds of our Templar depression, and that we shall see more courageous and valiant Knights marching under the banner of our beloved Emmanuel, willing to wield their swords in the defense of the Christian Religion.[15]

Hope was in the air indeed by 1934 as Franklin Delano Roosevelt's "New Deal" was getting underway. However, it would take America's entry into the Second World War to bring more solid footing to the country financially.

After a period of rearmament in violation of the Treaty of Versailles, Germany invaded Poland in 1939; thus thrusting the European continent into war for a second time in the Twentieth Century.[16] With war the country began to retool for defense production and financial security was returning; all of the Commanderies of Oklahoma were able to make their per capita tax payments in 1941.[17] All across the country men were turning out to serve their country. Oklahoma would ultimately become home to a number of pilot and infantry training fields.[18] With this surge of men entering the service, there was renewed interest in fraternalism. William C. Gordon, Grand Junior Warden of the Grand Encampment took note of this in his address to the Sir Knights of Oklahoma in 1941 and remarked:

> We are a semi-military organization. It is rather a military age in this country at this time. We ought to be thinking about increasing the number of young men in the Commandery…[19]

The military aspect of the Order certainly appealed to military men. Though not a young man, Ewell Lewis Head had served as commanding officer of the 180th Infantry headquartered at Muskogee.[20] Throughout the 1940s, he served as a field drill competition judge and was a member of the Work & Tactics Committee.[21] Grand Commander Marvin A. Wilson even had the honor of knighting his son, Staff Sergeant M.A. Wilson of the 13th Airborne.[22] This "war boom" generated the creation of 110 new Sir Knights in 1942, the largest number created since 1930.[23] By 1944 the tide was beginning to turn as membership had risen from its lowest point to 3,336 Sir Knights.[24] Just as everyone was doing their part to help win the war, so did the Sir Knights of Oklahoma. It was noted in 1943 that 136 Sir Knights were in the military and 200 more engaged in defense work of some fashion.[25]

War also called for sacrifices and the Templars in Oklahoma were not exempt. General Order No. 7 in 1942 suspended some activities that were the highlights of the Grand Conclave. Grand Commander Ernest C. Lambert remarked:

> Because our beloved country is faced with an extreme emergency requiring the use of all our energy, time, and resources for the preservation of Justice, Truth, Liberty,

General Ewell Lewis Head on the Drill Field
Courtesy of David Greenshields

Grand Commandery Officers in 1943
Courtesy of the Grand Commandery of Oklahoma

Democracy, and the Christian Religion and because the interests of our Great Order are identical with those of our country, I hereby declare an emergency exists.

After consulting with the Grand Officers and many Past Grand Commanders and members of the Grand Commandery, it has been decided to dispense with all competitive drills, the parade, and Grand Commander's Ball for this Annual Conclave.[26]

This suspension of activities carried over to the Grand Encampment as only eight Sir Knights from Oklahoma attended the Triennial in 1943 at Chicago where no grand parade was held and only business transacted. Even the widely seen corner stone ceremonies were set aside during the war.[27] Production during World War II shifted from general consumer goods to defense. Automobile factories were turning out tanks and bombers instead of passenger vehicles. In 1943 the manufacture of uniforms was prohibited by the War Production Board and new Templar uniforms could not be had.[28] The annual session of the Grand Commandery of Oklahoma even had to be postponed in 1945 due to restrictions placed on meetings of fifty or more by the Office of Defense Transportation.[29]

As Grand Commander Marvin A. Wilson noted in 1945, "In less than four years – short years as time is reckoned, but long years for mothers, sisters, and wives – the might of right and justice brought defeat, complete and unconditional, to the 'superior' races of the East and West."[30] It was determined that readjustment was to commence at once in the wake of the war's end so that Templary could regain all the lost ground possible.[31] A veritable revival was underway and by 1949 there were 4,832 Sir Knights in Oklahoma.[32] Unfortunately, five Commanderies ceased to exist during the 1950s.[33] Interestingly enough when Grand Officers arrived in Pawhuska to arrest the charter of Palestine No. 35, no Sir Knights could be found to relinquish their records.[34] While the Order was undergoing a rebirth, Grand Commander Ansel M. Crowder truly grasped the situation in regards to lost Commanderies. He remarked:

> As a general of the army shortens to strengthen his lines, so have we shortened, and I doubt not, strengthened our potential ability to secure petitions…[35]

By 1959 the total membership of the Grand Commandery stood at 5,564 Sir Knights, a 76% increase since the low of 1943.[36]

The Great Depression and the Second World War created hard times for many, the Sir Knights included, but the need for charitable giving persisted. In 1936 the Grand Chapter appropriated $12,000 to erect a vocational school at the Masonic Children's Home in Guthrie.[37] The Grand Chapter of the Eastern Star in turn donated $5,000 to equip the building for instruction. To the dismay of the Sir Knights, the Grand Commandery lacked the funds to donate as a group. It was Past Grand Commander Harold B. Downing who presented the idea of his fellow Sir Knights making individual donations to be collected for equipping the vocational school. Grand Recorder James A. Lathim was tasked with collecting donations and recommended that the Sir Knights each contribute a dollar.[38] The constituent Commanderies each involved themselves with local charity whenever possible. In 1940 Enid No. 13 distributed food baskets to the needy and Oklahoma No. 3 contributed to the Salvation Army.[39] Across the Nation, Grand Commanderies were taking up the banner of the Hospitalers Movement to coordinate charitable activity. Some of the aims of the movement were visits to the sick and shut-ins, foods baskets for the poor, and to find employment for Sir Knights.[40] Masonic Service Centers were established in both Lawton and Muskogee during the War, two hubs of military activity in the State. In 1944 the Grand Commandery provided the center in Lawton with kitchen equipment, while Muskogee received a billiard table.[41] Out of some seventy Masonic Service Centers across the country, Muskogee's was rated as the second best.[42] Other donations to those in service included 2,500 Bibles by Enid No. 13 and Gethsemane No. 25.[43] While the Grand Encampment had previously engaged in national philanthropies, in 1955 they took up the business of medical research and indigent care with the Knight Templar Eye Foundation. The Sir Knights were each to contribute one dollar a year to fund the new philanthropy.[44]

The Masonic Service Center at Lawton during World War II
Courtesy of T.S. Akers

In the face of adversity, the Sir Knights of Oklahoma carried on. Having been established in the Twenties, the annual drill competition had become a major event for the Order. While the membership was suffering, the Grand Commandery made every attempt to maintain business as usual. Though the parades of the annual Grand Conclave were suspended during World War II, they were kept up during the Depression years. In 1933 there was a "regimental review" of eight Oklahoma drill teams.[45] The constituent Commanderies also kept up their tradition of parading as in 1934 four separate Commanderies secured dispensations to parade in public.[46] It was during the Thirties that the Sir Knights of Gethsemane Commandery No. 25 began to make a name for themselves on the drill field. In 1931 Gethsemane appeared in the drill competition of the 38th Triennial Conclave of the Grand Encampment at Minneapolis. It was there that Gethsemane took Third Place.[47] The following year Gethsemane was invited to the conclave of the Grand Commandery of Texas to parade and perform a drill exhibition.[48] The Sir Knights who comprised the Gethsemane drill team were so proficient on the drill field that in 1935 they served as the field drill judges for the Grand Commandery of Texas.[49] Other Commanderies also fielded drill teams at Triennials. At the 41st Triennial in Cleveland, the Sir Knights of Lawton No. 18 earned Fourth Place.[50] In 1946 Lawton No. 18, Trinity No. 20, Elk City No. 22, and Bethlehem No. 45 all sent drill teams to the Triennial in Houston; with Lawton again taking Fourth Place.[51] At Indianapolis in 1958 a night parade of twenty-two drill teams was held. Two of those teams were fielded by Lawton and Gethsemane who both placed in their respective classes.[52] Lawton No. 18 was even featured in a "Templar Film" exhibiting the Long Form Opening and Manual of the Sword under the direction of Past Grand Commander John I. Taylor.[53]

Through the years the constituent Commanderies instituted a number of social activities to enhance the Templar year. By 1935 Trinity No. 20 was holding an annual ball for the Sir Knights and their Ladies of Tulsa.[54] The Annual Conclave of the Grand Commandery at this time also included a ball in addition to the grand banquet. The 1949 Grand Commander's Ball was held in the beautiful Crystal Ballroom of the Mayo Hotel in Tulsa.[55] In

Gethsemane Commandery No. 25, Third Place at 39th Triennial in 1931

Courtesy of the Grand Commandery of Oklahoma

Opening Parade of the Annual Conclave of the Grand Commandery in 1948

Courtesy of the Grand Commandery of Oklahoma

1937 a conclave was held in Guthrie for the purpose of conferring all of the Commandery Orders.[56] It was proposed that this degree conferral be held in conjunction with the Grand Chapter and Council. The "Fall Festival" would be continued and by 1938 twenty-one of forty-two Commanderies were participating.[57] It was noted in 1940 that Muskogee No. 2 held five dinner parties for its membership and Lawton No. 18 was participating in the "famous" Wichita Mountains Easter Pageant.[58] Hugo No. 30 had developed fraternal relations with their Brother Sir Knights across the Red River in Texas and on May 27, 1944, a joint conclave was held with Paris No. 9 in which 105 Sir Knights were in attendance.[59] One event that had become a standing tradition was the Good Friday Meeting of Trinity No. 20 in Tulsa. The meeting itself had been created by Past Grand Commanders Richard E. Newhouse and Hal F. Rambo and was an event known throughout the State. Sir Knights gathered annually for a special conferral of the Order of the Temple by a team composed of Past Commanders from across Oklahoma. Special lighting effects were used to enhance the ritual work and all of the Sir Knights that formed the lines for the knighting were Past Grand Commanders.[60] The year 1945 marked the 50th anniversary of the Grand Commandery of Oklahoma and the first "Fifty Year" member was present; Jesse Lee Blakemore had been knighted in Muskogee in 1895.[61]

It was at the 53rd Annual Conclave of the Grand Commandery that the Sir Knights of Oklahoma took a step towards modernity by adopting a new uniform.[62] Old traditions die hard and this change was by all accounts a long time coming. The Knights Templar regalia, or uniform as it would become, had undergone three major evolutions in the United States. In those early days, the Knights Templar degree, or Order of the Temple as it is properly known, was largely unregulated and the regalia used for the ritual even more so. The earliest element of Templar Regalia is the apron, which was generally black, often triangular in design, and nearly always featured a skull & crossbones along with crossed swords.[63] As the Templar degrees were originally being worked in Blue Lodges, it is possible that the aprons being worn were simply modified Blue Lodge aprons.[64] In 1859 the Grand Encampment of Knights Templar of the United States finally took up the banner of standardizing the regalia of the Order.[65] While far from the standards of Prussia, America at the time was very much a militaristic society. Every town at the time maintained a local militia and some even boasted more than one. Prior to the American Civil War these militias were merely social groups that would gather once a week to drill in uniform and impress the ladies.[66] It was common for more affluent units to adopt expensive European uniforms and men of less means, who wanted to impress the ladies themselves, would then form their own units and adopt a uniform that the only matching item might be a shirt of the same color.[67] The uniform adopted by the Grand Encampment in 1859 consisted of a white surcoat without sleeves worn over a black coat, a red leather belt, all worn with gauntlets, sword, and chapeau.[68] This first "uniform" was more of a costume than a uniform but did bear one very stylistic piece of military fashion, a chapeau. The chapeau, which is short for chapeau-de-bras, or cocked hat (the hat could be folded flat and tucked under the arm) had been in military service since the early 1800s.[69]

    The Grand Encampment again revised the uniform in 1862 and this time it took a more distinctly military look. In 1841 the United States Army adopted the Model-1841 Undress Frockcoat. This consisted of a form fitting jacket with standing collar that came to the waist and had a lower "skirt" that extended to the knee.[70] In time this would become the standard dress uniform, and field uniform in certain variations, of the United States Army, the Confederate States Army in 1861, and the style was adopted in some form by many militaries of the world. The Knights Templar uniform as adopted in 1862 consisted of the now in vogue military frockcoat, shoulder straps in the same form as the United States Army, chapeau, and sword. Manufacturer surpluses due to war production helped to make the new uniform readily available.[71] This uniform would serve the Sir Knights of the United States in some form for over 140 years. The uniform's lasting power was not only limited to the Knights Templar. If one were to compare the full dress uniform of United States Army Officers in 1890 to those of Knights Templar at the same time, they would find them to be nearly identical.[72] The United States Army would continue to wear the frockcoat as a full dress uniform until 1936 when a

General John M. Schofield, c. 1890
Courtesy of T.S. Akers

Unknown Sir Knight, c. 1890
Courtesy of T.S. Akers

Visitors to the Grand Commandery of Oklahoma in 1946
exhibiting the three types of Templar uniforms of the era
Courtesy of the Grand Commandery of Oklahoma

single breasted short coat with notched lapel, known as the Model-1936, was adopted.[73] The Knights Templar of Oklahoma would soldier on in their 19th Century uniforms until 1948. It had been noted that it was hard to gain new members while wearing "Civil War uniforms" and if one compares photos of Sir Knights in 1948 to those of 1949, it is like stepping back in time one hundred years. The uniform that was adopted in 1948 strays from the army tradition into naval territory. The new uniform consisted of a short coat with notched lapel, but it was double breasted – similar to that of a naval officer.[74] The chapeau remained, now considered traditional and thereby irremovable, and the Sir Knight took on the look of a seafaring man.[75]

The end of the Second World War would see one evil vanquished only to be replaced by a new threat. The United States had a very unlikely ally in the Soviets during the War and some were very suspicious of them altogether. One notable critic of the Russians was General George S. Patton who believed they were devious and stated "… the Russian has no regard for human life and is an all out son of bitch, barbarian, and chronic drunk."[76] Patton was not alone in his sentiments concerning the Russians and the fear of communism. As Joseph Stalin rose to power he attacked the Christian Religion and to many Americans, and specifically Knights Templar, this attack was of major concern. Mahlon F. Manville, Grand Master of Masons of Oklahoma, appealed to the vows of the Sir Knights to defend the Christian Religion in 1933. He remarked:

> Soviet Russia has decreed that by May 4, 1934, all churches and houses of prayer are to be closed in every capital in that country and by May 1, 1937, the very conception of God shall be banished from the land.
>
> …The Knights Templar by teaching and tradition should be the shock troops. Each one should gird up his loins, strap to his thigh the sword we vowed to wield for the cause of the Christian faith and go out and meet the enemy.[77]

To many, the threat of communism posed by Soviet Russia was very real. In 1946 Winston Churchill stated that an "iron curtain" had descended across Eastern Europe.[78] By 1950 America would

Grand Commandery Officers in 1950
Courtesy of the Grand Commandery of Oklahoma

enter into the Korean War and a policy of containment of communism was enacted.[79] It was Senator Joseph McCarthy who led a personal attack on suspected communists in the United States during the Fifties.[80] While inwardly there was no question that the Knights Templar fully supported the country in which they resided, outwardly in a time of fear they could quite easily be considered a dangerous para-military organization. It was likely due to this that the Patriotic Activities Committee was established in 1952.[81]

Patriotic Activities placed into one category a variety of activities in which the Sir Knights of Oklahoma had already been concerning themselves. These included support of youth activities, contributions to blood banks, work with the Red Cross, civilian defense work, and encouraging service in the armed forces by Sir Knights.[82] In addition to reporting their general Templar activities of the year, the constituent Commanderies now were to report their "Patriotic Activities." It was noted in 1953 that Ardmore No. 9 helped provide instruments to the Children's Salvation Army Band.[83] Norman No. 38 fulfilled their obligation by promoting the Knights Templar Education Fund on the campus of the University of Oklahoma.[84] Of course nothing could be more patriotic than supporting the George Washington Masonic Memorial being constructed in Alexandria, Virginia. In 1956 it was decided that $0.15 would be given by each Sir Knight in the United States to furnish a chapel in the Memorial.[85] Visitors to the Memorial today find a wonderfully equipped chapel in the Gothic style situated in the tower. The room is accentuated with four stained glass windows depicting scenes from the life of Jesus.[86]

The years that followed the roaring Twenties truly were years of doubt and despair. The world was suffering a drastic economic downturn. War would again tear the European continent apart. In peace came a new threat as serious as that imposed by the Axis Powers during World War II. Amidst all of this, the Sir Knights of Oklahoma steadily marched forward through time. A membership depleted by the Depression found renewed interest in fraternalism. The close of the 1950s saw Templary in Oklahoma advancing into a modern era in a position of strength.

Notes

[1] Robert H. Frank and Ben S. Bernanke, *Principles of Macroeconomics* (Boston: McGraw-Hill, 2007), 98.

[2] "Dust Bowl," Oklahoma Historical Society's Encyclopedia of Oklahoma History and Culture, <http://digital.library.okstate.edu/encyclopedia/entries/D/DU011.html>, Accessed 18 June 2012.

[3] Grand Commandery of Knights Templar of Oklahoma, *Proceedings of the 35th Annual Conclave* (Oklahoma: 1930).

[4] Grand Commandery of Knights Templar of Oklahoma, *Proceedings of the 36th Annual Conclave* (Oklahoma: 1931).

[5] Ibid.

[6] Grand Commandery of Knights Templar of Oklahoma, *Proceedings of the 37th Annual Conclave* (Oklahoma: 1932).

[7] Grand Commandery of Knights Templar of Oklahoma, *Proceedings of the 36th Annual Conclave*.

[8] Grand Commandery of Knights Templar of Oklahoma, *Proceedings of the 84th Annual Conclave* (Oklahoma: 1979).

[9] Grand Commandery of Knights Templar of Oklahoma, *Proceedings of the 39th Annual Conclave* (Oklahoma: 1934).

[10] Grand Commandery of Knights Templar of Oklahoma, *Proceedings of the 41st Annual Conclave* (Oklahoma: 1936).

[11] Grand Commandery of Knights Templar of Oklahoma, *Proceedings of the 42nd Annual Conclave* (Oklahoma: 1937).

[12] Grand Commandery of Knights Templar of Oklahoma, *Proceedings of the 45th Annual Conclave* (Oklahoma: 1940).

[13] "A Pictorial Tour of the Center," McAlester Scottish Rite Center, <http://www.mcalesterscottishrite.org/Auditorium.htm >, Accessed 18 June 2012.

[14] Gene McKelvey, *The Masonic History of the Murrah Building Bombing Memorial Museum* (Oklahoma: The Oklahoma Lodge of Research), 5-6.

[15] Grand Commandery of Knights Templar of Oklahoma, *Proceedings of the 39th Annual Conclave*.

[16] "World War II," History.com, <http://www.history.com/topics/world-war-ii>, Accessed 1 July 2012.

[17] Grand Commandery of Knights Templar of Oklahoma, *Proceedings of the 46th Annual Conclave* (Oklahoma: 1941).

[18] "Camp Gruber," Oklahoma Historical Society's Encyclopedia of Oklahoma History and Culture, <http://digital.library.okstate.edu/encyclopedia/entries/C/CA022.html >, Accessed 19 June 2012.

[19] Grand Commandery of Knights Templar of Oklahoma, *Proceedings of the 46th Annual Conclave*.

[20] Oklahoma Military Department, *Historical Annual National Guard of the State of Oklahoma 1938* (Baton Rouge, Louisiana: Army and Navy Publishing Co., 1938), 41.

[21] Grand Commandery of Knights Templar of Oklahoma, *Proceedings of the 46th Annual Conclave*.

[22] Grand Commandery of Knights Templar of Oklahoma, *Proceedings of the 50th Annual Conclave* (Oklahoma: 1945).

[23] Grand Commandery of Knights Templar of Oklahoma, *Proceedings of the 47th Annual Conclave* (Oklahoma: 1942).

[24] Grand Commandery of Knights Templar of Oklahoma, *Proceedings of the 49th Annual Conclave* (Oklahoma: 1944).

[25] Grand Commandery of Knights Templar of Oklahoma, *Proceedings of the 48th Annual Conclave* (Oklahoma: 1943).

[26] Grand Commandery of Knights Templar of Oklahoma, *Proceedings of the 47th Annual Conclave*.

[27] Grand Commandery of Knights Templar of Oklahoma, *Proceedings of the 49th Annual Conclave*.

[28] Grand Commandery of Knights Templar of Oklahoma, *Proceedings of the 48th Annual Conclave*.

[29] Grand Commandery of Knights Templar of Oklahoma, *Proceedings of the 50th Annual Conclave*.

[30] Ibid.

[31] Grand Commandery of Knights Templar of Oklahoma, *Proceedings of the 51st Annual Conclave* (Oklahoma: 1946).

[32] Grand Commandery of Knights Templar of Oklahoma, *Proceedings of the 54th Annual Conclave* (Oklahoma: 1949).

[33] Grand Commandery of Knights Templar of Oklahoma, *Proceedings of the 84th Annual Conclave* (Oklahoma: 1979).

[34] Grand Commandery of Knights Templar of Oklahoma, *Proceedings of the 59th Annual Conclave* (Oklahoma: 1954).

[35] Grand Commandery of Knights Templar of Oklahoma, *Proceedings of the 60th Annual Conclave* (Oklahoma: 1955).

[36] Grand Commandery of Knights Templar of Oklahoma, *Proceedings of the 64th Annual Conclave* (Oklahoma: 1959).

[37] Norman E. Angel, Kenneth S. Adams, and William A. Hensley, *History of the Grand Chapter of the Royal Arch Masons of Oklahoma* (Oklahoma: 1964), 48.

[38] Grand Commandery of Knights Templar of Oklahoma, *Proceedings of the 41st Annual Conclave*.

[39] Grand Commandery of Knights Templar of Oklahoma, *Proceedings of the 45th Annual Conclave*.

[40] Grand Commandery of Knights Templar of Oklahoma, *Proceedings of the 47th Annual Conclave*.

[41] Grand Commandery of Knights Templar of Oklahoma, *Proceedings of the 49th Annual Conclave*.

[42] Grand Commandery of Knights Templar of Oklahoma, *Proceedings of the 51st Annual Conclave*.

[43] Grand Commandery of Knights Templar of Oklahoma, *Proceedings of the 50th Annual Conclave*.

[44] Grand Commandery of Knights Templar of Oklahoma, *Proceedings of the 56th Annual Conclave* (Oklahoma: 1951).

[45] Grand Commandery of Knights Templar of Oklahoma, *Proceedings of the 38th Annual Conclave* (Oklahoma: 1933).

[46] Grand Commandery of Knights Templar of Oklahoma, *Proceedings of the 39th Annual Conclave*.

[47] Grand Commandery of Knights Templar of Oklahoma, *Proceedings of the 37th Annual Conclave*.

[48] Grand Commandery of Knights Templar of Oklahoma, *Proceedings of the 39th Annual Conclave*.

[49] Grand Commandery of Knights Templar of Oklahoma, *Proceedings of the 40th Annual Conclave* (Oklahoma: 1935).

[50] Grand Commandery of Knights Templar of Oklahoma, *Proceedings of the 46th Annual Conclave*.

[51] Grand Commandery of Knights Templar of Oklahoma, *Proceedings of the 52nd Annual Conclave* (Oklahoma: 1947).

[52] Grand Commandery of Knights Templar of Oklahoma, *Proceedings of the 64th Annual Conclave*.

[53] Grand Commandery of Knights Templar of Oklahoma, *Proceedings of the 46th Annual Conclave*.

[54] Grand Commandery of Knights Templar of Oklahoma, *Proceedings of the 40th Annual Conclave*.

[55] Grand Commandery of Knights Templar of Oklahoma, *Proceedings of the 54th Annual Conclave*.

[56] Grand Commandery of Knights Templar of Oklahoma, *Proceedings of the 42nd Annual Conclave*.

[57] Grand Commandery of Knights Templar of Oklahoma, *Proceedings of the 44th Annual Conclave* (Oklahoma: 1939).

[58] Grand Commandery of Knights Templar of Oklahoma, *Proceedings of the 45th Annual Conclave*.

[59] Grand Commandery of Knights Templar of Oklahoma, *Proceedings of the 50th Annual Conclave*.

[60] Grand Commandery of Knights Templar of Oklahoma, *Proceedings of the 53rd Annual Conclave* (Oklahoma: 1948).

[61] Grand Commandery of Knights Templar of Oklahoma, *Proceedings of the 50th Annual Conclave*.

[62] Grand Commandery of Knights Templar of Oklahoma, *Proceedings of the 53rd Annual Conclave* .

[63] Aimee E. Newell, "Inspired by Fashion: Knight Templar Regalia," *Knight Templar*, April 2012, 30.

[64] Ron Blaisdell, "A History of the Knights Templar Apron," *Knight Templar*, August 1989.

[65] Newell, 31.

[66] Ibid, 28.

[67] Editors of Time-Life Books, *Echoes of Glory: Arms and Equipment of The Union* (Alexandria, Virginia: Time-Life Books, 1998), 92-97.

[68] Newell, 31.

[69] H.A. Ogden, *Uniforms of the United States Army: 1774-1889* (Mineola, New York: Dover Publications, Inc., 1998), Plate 12.

[70] Ibid, Plate 18.

[71] Newell, 28-33.

[72] Ogden, Plate 39.

[73] Shelby Stanton, *U.S. Army Uniforms of World War II* (Mechanicsburg, Pennsylvania: Stackpole Books, 1991), 16.

[74] Grand Commandery of Knights Templar of Oklahoma, *Proceedings of the 53rd Annual Conclave*.

[75] Newell, 33.

[76] Stanley P. Hirshson, *General Patton : A Soldier's Life* (New York: HarperCollins, 2003), 650.

[77] Grand Commandery of Knights Templar of Oklahoma, *Proceedings of the 38th Annual Conclave*.

[78] Robert R. James, *Winston S. Churchill: His Complete Speeches 1897-1963* (New York and London: Chelsea House Publishers, 1974), Vol. 7: 7285-7293.

[79] "Korean War," History.com, <http://www.history.com/topics/korean-war>, Accessed July 1 2012.

[80] "Joseph R. McCarthy, History.com, <http://www.history.com/topics/joseph-mccarthy>, Accessed July 1 2012.

[81] Grand Commandery of Knights Templar of Oklahoma, *Proceedings of the 57th Annual Conclave* (Oklahoma: 1952).

[82] Ibid.

[83] Grand Commandery of Knights Templar of Oklahoma, *Proceedings of the 58th Annual Conclave* (Oklahoma: 1953).

[84] Grand Commandery of Knights Templar of Oklahoma, *Proceedings of the 60th Annual Conclave*.

[85] Grand Commandery of Knights Templar of Oklahoma, *Proceedings of the 61st Annual Conclave* (Oklahoma: 1956).

[86] "Interactive Tour of the Memorial," The George Washington Masonic Memorial, <http://gwmemorial.org/tour.php>, Accessed 1 July 2012.

IV: Decline and Renewal

It was war that brought men to the Fraternity after the Great Depression and it was war that ultimately kept them from coming to the Fraternity in the decades immediately following the close of the 1950s. By 1960 the country was experiencing economic prosperity and the middle class was gaining ground. With prosperity came increased leisure time and the youth used this to take up such causes as civil rights, women's rights, and a rejection of the Vietnam War; which had initially experienced widespread support.[1] Thus the counterculture movement was born and a whole generation rejected the standards their parents had set forth in the preceding years.[2] For the next forty years the Fraternity would see a steady decline in membership and the Knights Templar were not exempt. In time, a renewed interest in American fraternalism would begin; a renewed interest that has steadily gained momentum.

After thirty years without any new Commanderies being chartered and a number of Commanderies ceasing to exist, the early days of the 1960s showed promise. Interest in the Knights Templar was once again present in Atoka in 1960 and Grand Commander Milton McCullough saw fit to restore their charter.[3] Now working as No. 50, Hugh de Payen was reborn after originally consolidating with Ada No. 16 in 1939.[4] After years of York Rite Masonry in Guymon, the Sir Knights residing there who long had to leave Oklahoma to participate in Templary finally secured a dispensation to open their own Commandery. With a total of seventy-two members, Guymon Commandery No. 51 was chartered on April 25, 1961.[5] As the 1960s progressed the counterculture gained in popularity and Freemasonry saw fewer men coming to its doors. A life membership of $75 was created in

Guymon Commandery No. 51 in 1961
Courtesy of the Grand Commandery of Oklahoma

1962 to curb further membership losses.[6] This gave way to "perpetual memberships" which were established in 1986 as an investment option for constituent Commanderies so that a Sir Knights' dues would continue to benefit his home Commandery in interest earned after his passing.[7] The year 1964 saw the creation of a "Membership Award Program" in order to encourage Sir Knights to recruit new members.[8] The program saw its share of successes as eighty-five Sir Knights were knighted the following year in the John I. Taylor Memorial Class.[9]

It was in 1971 that Carl B. Albert, the "Little Giant from Little Dixie," was dubbed and created a Knight of the Temple. The fall degree conferral that year was styled the Carl Albert York Rite Festival and a total of 349 candidates took the degrees and orders of the York Rite. The class also boasted two other Oklahoma Congressmen, John "Happy" Camp and Ed Edmondson.[10] Unfortunately, the number of Sir Knights lost each year, either by death, suspension, or withdrawal, was outrunning the number knighted. In 1965 there were 5,207 Sir Knights in Oklahoma.[11] By 1970 the membership had dropped to 4,283 Sir Knights.[12] Again Commanderies were facing a grave situation and many closed their doors forever. On January 19, 1965, Ascension No. 4 at El Reno, one of the original three Commanderies of Oklahoma, merged with Oklahoma No. 3. Drumright No. 47 was forced to consolidate with Cushing No. 42 and by 1978 Cushing voted to move their charter to Drumright, thus returning Templary to that city under the name Cimarron Valley.[13] In 1979 the newly restored Hugh de Payen No. 50 at Atoka lost their charter for the final time.[14] After years without growth, 1989 saw two new Commanderies chartered; Tipton No. 52 and Capitol Hill No. 53.[15] Sadly, the years following 1989 saw more Commanderies stricken from the rolls. As some closed and others consolidated with nearby Commanderies, a small group of strong Commanderies rose from the ashes like the phoenix. Today in Oklahoma there are sixteen active Commanderies as follows:

Guthrie No. 1	at Guthrie
Muskogee No. 2	at Muskogee
Oklahoma No. 3	at Oklahoma City

Carl Albert York Rite Festival in 1971
Courtesy of the Grand Commandery of Oklahoma

The Honorable Carl B. Albert is seated sixth from the right on the front row.

McAlester No. 6	at McAlester
St. Johns No. 8	at Stillwater
Ardmore No. 9	at Ardmore
Ben Hur No. 14	at Ponca City
Lawton No. 18	at Lawton
Trinity No. 20	at Tulsa
Elk City No. 22	at Elk City
Gethsemane No. 25	at Okmulgee
Calvary No. 26	at Bartlesville
St. Aumer No. 29	at Woodward
Norman No. 38	at Norman
Cimarron Valley No. 42	at Drumright
Capitol Hill No. 53	at Midwest City[16]

While the latter half of the twentieth century saw the numbers that had comprised Templary in Oklahoma shrink, the Sir Knights soldiered on with the various activities of the Order.

The late Fifties and early Sixties saw the Sir Knights of Oklahoma return to the Grand Encampment Stage. At the 46th Triennial, the Grand Encampment divided its jurisdiction up into Departments.[17] It was in 1958 that Past Grand Commander Oliver S. Willham was appointed as the first Right Eminent Department Commander from Oklahoma.[18] As Willham's term as an officer of the Grand Encampment was winding down, another Oklahoma Sir Knight was hoping to begin his journey to the apex of Templary. Past Grand Commander William E. Crowe made himself available for Grand Generalissimo of the Grand Encampment in 1961. While he was not successful in his bid for office, Crowe was appointed Chair of the Grand Encampment Jurisprudence Committee.[19] Oklahoma would see two more Sir Knights serve as Right Eminent Department Commander; Clell C. Warriner in 1973 and James C. Taylor in 1994.[20] It was in 1967 that another of Oklahoma's own held office with the Grand Encampment. The Reverend Canon Curtis W.V. Junker of Tulsa served as Grand Prelate for the 50th Triennial.[21]

Past Right Eminent Department Commander Clell C. Warriner receiving his Fifty Year Pin from his son Joe Warriner in 1983

Courtesy of the Grand Commandery of Oklahoma

Oklahoma had three long serving Grand Recorders. The first was George W. Spencer who served for 29 years commencing in 1905. The second, James A. Lathim of Muskogee began his 28 years of service in 1934. Lathim was followed by Fritz M. Lumbard in 1963; Lumbard would serve for 18 years and was made an Honorary Past Grand Commander of Oklahoma.[22] The year 1971 would see a special event held to honor one Oklahoma Mason in particular. Leslie Swan became the first Oklahoman to earn four quadrants for his Knight of the York Cross of Honour jewel (the KYCH as it is known is an invitational York Rite body requiring its members to have served as presiding officer of a Symbolic Lodge, Chapter of Royal Masons, Council of Cryptic Masons, and Commandery of Knights Templar). Swan held the office of Grand Master in 1922, Grand Commander in 1929, Grand High Priest in 1931, and Grand Illustrious Master in 1934.[23] Swan was called home to the celestial Lodge above a few short years later in 1975.[24] The Masons of Oklahoma of course celebrated the accomplishments of noteworthy Brethren whenever possible. In 1990 country performer Roy Clark was dubbed and created a Knight of the Temple in a special festival celebrating the centennial of the Grand Chapter of Royal Arch Masons of Oklahoma and as such "one hundred years of York Rite Masonry in Oklahoma." There were five hundred members and candidates in attendance at the banquet held to mark the occasion at the Doubletree Hotel in Tulsa.[25]

Banquets and parades are of course the standard means of Masonic celebration and this period was no exception. There were four dispensations granted to Commanderies to parade in 1966.[26] Harkening back to the memory of the ancient Templars, Grand Commander Frederick J. Smith conducted a special feast in 1967 to commemorate the adoption of the *Regula Templariorum* at the Council of Troyes in 1129.[27] The Sir Knights of Oklahoma also took an active part in the Bi-Centennial of the Nation; Bethlehem No. 45 participated in the Freedom Festival Parade on July 2nd in Del City, the American Heritage Parade on July 3rd in Oklahoma City, and a joint program with Amity Lodge No. 473 on July 4th.[28] With parading came the need for drill and the annual drill competition was maintained until the early 2000s. In 1976 Gethsemane No. 25 placed second at the Triennial drill

Grand Recorder George W. Spencer, serving from 1905 to 1933
Courtesy of the Grand Commander of Oklahoma

Grand Recorder James A. Lathim, serving from 1934 to 1962
Courtesy of the Grand Commandery of Oklahoma

competition in Kansas City, Missouri.[29] The prominence of Gethsemane was such that in time the Statewide Drill Team of Oklahoma would march under Gethsemane's banner.[30] The Statewide Drill Team would come to be sponsored by the Oklahoma Past Commanders Association, the association having been formed in 1972.[31] The team first paraded under the sponsorship of the Past Commander's Association in 1988 with eighteen Sir Knights in the Frontier Days Parade in Tecumseh; Past Grand Commander James C. Taylor served as Drill Captain. In an effort to encourage participation by smaller Commanderies, a Class D drill team was demonstrated at Norman in 1988; a "D Team" only required seven Sir Knights.[32] For a number of years, there were no drill teams competing in Oklahoma. It was at the 60th Triennial of the Grand Encampment in St. Louis that the Oklahoma Statewide Drill Team placed fifth in the drill competition.[33] By 2000, drill teams in Oklahoma were far and few between with only an exhibition drill occurring at the annual conclave of the Grand Commandery.[34] The last drill competition was held in 2003 with two Class C drill teams competing, Trinity No. 20 and Elk City No. 22; the two teams were to combine for the trek to the Triennial that year.[35]

One could refer to the period commencing with the 1960s and spanning to today the modern era of Templary. Throughout this period the need for charitable giving persisted as it had previously. The recently formed Knights Templar Eye Foundation was gaining ground and in 1966 the Sir Knights of Oklahoma raised $4,916 for the foundation; the top three donators were Trinity No. 20 with $596, Muskogee No. 2 with $585, and Oklahoma No. 3 with $550.[36] The Sir Knights faithfully gave to the Eye Foundation throughout the years and in 2003 the Grand Commandery of Oklahoma partnered with the Dean A. McGee Eye Institute in Oklahoma City. In 2009 the Foundation provided $270,848 in eye care for indigent Oklahomans through the Dean A. McGee Eye Institute.[37] Donations for the Knights Templar Eye Foundation from Oklahoma totaled nearly $12,000 in 2010, illustrating the importance of the Foundation to the Sir Knights.[38] To date, the Foundation has presented a number of research grants, each in excess of $30,000, to researchers at the Dean A. McGee Eye Institute.[39]

Members of the Work and Tactics Committee in 1986
Courtesy of the Grand Commandery of Oklahoma

Gethsemane Commandery No. 25 Field Drill Team in 1989
Courtesy of the Grand Commandery of Oklahoma

Other causes that were maintained included the Educational Loan Fund as well as the continued support of the Order of DeMolay. By 1972 there was a total of $98,594 in outstanding student loans.[40] To several Grand Commanders, the pursuit of higher education was truly a passion. For example, Past Grand Commander Victor G. Heller served as the Agricultural Chemistry Research Chair at Oklahoma A&M in 1924.[41] Oliver S. Willham held the office of President of Oklahoma A&M from 1952 to 1966.[42] It was Grand Commander Richard B. Burch who secured the elevation of Cameron University to a four-year educational institution during his tenure as President from 1960 to 1969.[43] By 1999 educational loans were no longer being granted and thirty-seven loans were returned to the Grand Encampment to be dissolved.[44] To replace the old loan program, a scholarship program was adopted and today four scholarships of $1,250 each are given annually.[45] Donations to the Order of DeMolay generally averaged $500 to $700 a year.[46] In 1977 a leadership workshop was established for the youth order dubbed the "York Rite Workshop" which has continued to present day.[47] In 1982 the Order of Knighthood for the DeMolay Association was established to promote the York Rite to the "DeMolay Boys." Though not in existence today, the association gave a traveling trophy to the "Knight of the Year" and worked to educate the boys on what Masonry and Templary were.[48] At the 99th annual conclave of the Grand Commandery, the DeMolay Committee recommended that a Knights Templar sword be given to one outstanding DeMolay annually.[49] Though not approved until 1997, today the Grand Commandery of Oklahoma presents an official sword at the York Rite Workshop every winter.[50] While the York Rite as a whole has maintained support for all of the Masonic Youth groups in Oklahoma, charitable work for the youth of Oklahoma began with the Masonic Children's Home. Originally established at Darlington and later moved to Guthrie, the home closed in 1978.[51]

At the 56th Triennial of the Grand Encampment at Cincinnati, Ohio, a new charitable program was taken up. As the ancient Templars were founded to protect pilgrims in the Holy Land, it was deemed that it was time for a return to the Order's "ancient roots." The Holy Land Pilgrimage Committee was

Past Grand Commanders of Oklahoma in 1972
Courtesy of the Grand Commandery of Oklahoma

created by the Grand Commandery of Oklahoma, as directed by the Grand Encampment, for the purpose of sending ministers to tour the Holy Land.[52] Oklahoma was able to send their first minister as part of the program in 1986.[53] It was noted that it cost $1,372 to send a minister in those early years of the program and fortunately donations were keeping up with the cost.[54] While the costs for the Holy Land Pilgrimage program have risen, $2,006 was raised in 2002 alone and the Sir Knights of Oklahoma still enjoy the privilege of sending ministers to the Holy Land today.[55] Charitable giving as a whole has certainly not slacked off as charity is one of the grand characteristics of Templary. Presently, the Grand Commandery of Oklahoma has a seat on the board of the Masonic Charity Foundation of Oklahoma.[56] Through the Foundation, charitable giving by Masons in Oklahoma is done in a collective form for the greater good; for example, $337,644 was raised for the Murrah Family Relief Fund in the wake of the Murrah Federal Building bombing in 1995.[57]

In this modern era of Templary, the Grand Commandery of Oklahoma has certainly seen its share of hard times as membership has declined. The Order's survival has been largely due to what can be called the "York Rite Tradition." The Freemasonry that arrived in America came from England and Masonic tradition in England included the degree of Holy Royal Arch, and often Knight Templar. In time a system of degrees would develop in America under the heading York Rite, though truthfully this can easily be called the "American Rite."[58] The prominence of York Rite Masonry can easily be seen throughout Masonic history in America. For example, the most prominent Mason in America in the early 1800s was DeWitt Clinton, Governor of New York and General Grand High Priest of the General Grand Chapter of the United States. Clinton's opponent for his third term as General Grand High Priest happened to be a future president and Past Grand Master of Tennessee, Andrew Jackson.[59] Clinton would go on to serve as the first Most Excellent Grand Master of the Grand Encampment in 1816.[60] When Freemasonry arrived in what is today Oklahoma, those Brethren brought with them the early elements of York Rite Masonry. Recognizing the importance of the York Rite, it was "modern" Oklahoma Masons that ensured the Order's survival.

The men that were active in the creation of the Grand Bodies that would come to be the York Rite in Oklahoma, and more specifically the Grand Commandery of Knights Templar, were also active Scottish Rite Masons. When Harper S. Cunningham arrived in Guthrie as part of the Land Run of 1889, he just happened to serve on the Supreme Council of the Scottish Rite in Kansas.[61] What Cunningham also brought to the new Oklahoma Territory was his membership in the York Rite and he would become the first Grand Recorder of the Grand Commandery of Oklahoma; and five short years later, Grand Commander.[62] His prominence in Masonry was not limited to the York Rite though; Cunningham also served as the first Sovereign Grand Inspector General of the Scottish Rite in Oklahoma.[63] Through the years the two Rites marched side by side, their memberships growing in tandem. It was during the temple building period of the 1920s that this began to change. The Scottish Rite began to attract more members due to its embracement of the theater tradition and in time would become the "social center" of Freemasonry in Oklahoma. As the Depression took hold in the 1930s and Commanderies, as well as Chapters of Royal Arch Masons, began to close, the reach of the York Rite into local Blue Lodges diminished; while the reach of the Scottish Rite with its bi-annual Reunions remained constant. A weekend of fraternalism in Guthrie or McAlester twice a year was more feasible for many Masons during hard times than a monthly trip to their Commandery in a town that could be twenty-five to fifty miles away. For these reasons the membership of the York Rite began to suffer and an appearance of competition between the two Rites was born.[64]

In 1999 it was another Sovereign Grand Inspector General of Oklahoma that observed the perceived competition that existed among Masonic Bodies in the State and began to look for a way to correct it. Paul T. Million of McAlester began to push for unity of purpose and action in the State. He felt this could be achieved by coordinating schedules and providing space for degree work to be completed.[65] This was spurred on in February of 2000 when Million and Robert G. Davis, General Secretary of the Guthrie Valley of the Scottish Rite, saw the "Crusade 2000" program of the Grand Encampment as the perfect opportunity to re-establish

Installation of Grand Commandery Officers in 1998
Courtesy of the Grand Commandery of Oklahoma

the unity that had previously existed between the York and Scottish Rites. The first weekend in February saw "York Rite Field Days" held at all three Scottish Rite Temples in Oklahoma. A total of 246 Sir Knights were dubbed and created in this one day event with another 45 on a "follow up" day held in Guthrie.[66] The following year the Most Worshipful Grand Lodge of the State of Oklahoma officially moved to ensure unity among the Masonic Bodies in Oklahoma. Under the direction of Grand Master Robert T. Shipe, the Joint Agreement for Masonic Unity was signed establishing guidelines for scheduling and membership promotion between the Bodies.[67] Grand Master Shipe had previously spearheaded a York Rite presentation to encourage Masons to petition for membership.[68] In his address as Grand Commander, Robert G. Davis remarked on the re-established bond between the two Rites:

> There can be no fraternal or moral justification for jealousy and division between us because we are the heirs of a mutual heritage in our state. I will always promote membership, enthusiasm, and respect for both Rites because there are powerful and meaningful symbolic lessons and insights to be discovered in both. They were never meant to be mutually exclusive; and, indeed, to the true Masonic heart, should be so. Together, we offer unique and meaningful insights to the serious student of Masonry. His journey to mature masculinity is vastly facilitated by what we teach. I firmly believe we are essential to his well-being as a man. And, for the man of faith, the York Rite is certainly a profound fraternal affirmation of the nature of Brotherly love.[69]

After years of many Masons living under the belief that they need only belong to one Rite or the other as there was no reason to belong to both, the winds of change began to blow. Thus it was at the eleventh hour that the Grand Commandery of Oklahoma, and the York Rite as a whole, was saved and what is today a true "American Fraternal Society" lives on.[70]

Presently there is a renewed interest in Freemasonry in general and Templary in particular. This is due in part to recent books dealing with Freemasonry such as *The Lost Symbol* and films such as *National Treasure*. Indeed, the Fraternity often appears in

Grand Lodge Centennial Parade in 2009

Courtesy of Richard E. Massad and the Grand Lodge of the State of Oklahoma

Arch of Steel for Grand Master Massad in 2009

Courtesy of Richard E. Massad and the Grand Lodge of the State of Oklahoma

Annual Inspection of Capitol Hill Commandery No. 53 in 2012
Courtesy of Capitol Hill Commandery No. 53

Knight Templar Honor Guard at Sir Knight Akers' wedding
Courtesy of T.S. Akers

films today and many are intrigued by the perceived secrecy of Freemasonry. The renewed interest has even added to the notoriety of the Knights Templar. In recent years the Vatican has released several documents from the trials of the ancient Templars finding them innocent of the charges originally levied.[71] Though the membership today pales in comparison to the "Golden Age of Fraternalism," there is a spirit of revival for the Order in Oklahoma. It has been noted that both the Millennial Generation and the iGeneration possess an interest in Templary and quality fraternalism.[72] With the revival, the Sir Knights of Oklahoma have even been able to enjoy some of the traditional Templar activities. In November of 2007 the State of Oklahoma celebrated its Centennial and the Sir Knights of Oklahoma were on hand in force to parade.[73] Just two years later the Grand Commandery again made a parade appearance, this time for the Centennial celebration of the Most Worshipful Grand Lodge of the State of Oklahoma.[74] The Grand Commandery has long served as the ceremonial bodyguard of the Grand Master of Masons of Oklahoma and often affords him the Arch of Steel at the annual communication of the Grand Lodge.[75] With the renewed interest in Templary, in 2011 officers of the Grand Commandery assembled at the McAlester Scottish Rite Temple to serve as an honor guard at the wedding of one of their fellow officers.[76] The same year, under the direction of Grand Commander I. Dwayne Dixon, also saw every Commandery across Oklahoma actively engaged in Templary as all Commanderies stood Inspection for the first time in a number of years.[77]

    The revival of fraternalism led the Most Worshipful Grand Lodge of the State of Oklahoma to take one huge step forward in the late 2000s. In 1784 a warrant was issued to fifteen men in Boston, including one named Prince Hall, to form African Lodge No. 459 on the English Register. In time African Lodge declared itself the African Grand Lodge of Massachusetts in what was viewed as irregular fashion. For roughly two hundred years, the Prince Hall Grand Lodge of Massachusetts, as it is known today, spread Freemasonry amongst African-Americans across the United States independently of the predominately white Grand Lodges.[78] This segregated Masonry has only recently begun to fade. In 2010 the Grand Commandery of Oklahoma and the

Herman E. Duncan Grand Council and Commandery (Prince Hall Affiliated) acknowledged that their respective Grand Lodges had entered into a Compact providing for co-existence, respect of each other's absolute and supreme authority, and Masonic recognition.[79] This was followed on April 13, 2012, with Grand Commander Richard C. Dunaway signing a second Compact with Grand Commander Anthony E. Bowens of the Herman E. Duncan Ground Council and Grand Commandery providing for visitation by the Sir Knights between the two jurisdictions.[80] After many years, peace and harmony now prevails between the Sir Knights of Oklahoma and their Prince Hall counterparts.

Today the Grand Commandery of Knights Templar of Oklahoma is firmly rooted in the landscape of Freemasonry in what was once the "Twin Territories." Brethren in the Indian Territory were actively pursuing the "higher degrees" of Freemasonry prior to the 1890s. Sir Knights were present when the Oklahoma Territory was formed and when statehood came about, the Oklahoma Constitutional Convention boasted its fair share of Brethren. The Knights Templar in Oklahoma enjoyed the financial success of the Roaring Twenties and weathered the storm of the Great Depression. Even in the face of war and an entire generation of young men shunning fraternalism, the Grand Commandery of Oklahoma stood resolute. As Past Department Commander James C. Taylor promoted, "the preeminent mission of the Knights Templar is the support and defense of the Christian religion."[81] There is no doubt that the Sir Knights of Oklahoma will continue to carry that banner forth as they chart a course through the twenty-first century.

Grand Commander Richard C. Dunaway and Grand Commander Anthony E. Bowens signing the Compact for visitation

Courtesy of T.S. Akers

2012 Officers of the Grand Commandery Knights Templar of Oklahoma

Courtesy of Steven Guerrero

Notes

[1] Paul Krugman, *The Conscience of a Liberal* (New York: W.W. Norton & Co., 2007).

[2] Eric Donald Hirsch, *The Dictionary of Cultural Literacy* (Boston: Houghton Mifflin, 1993), 419.

[3] Grand Commandery of Knights Templar of Oklahoma, *Proceedings of the 65th Annual Conclave* (Oklahoma: 1960).

[4] Grand Commandery of Knights Templar of Oklahoma, *Proceedings of the 84th Annual Conclave* (Oklahoma: 1979).

[5] Grand Commandery of Knights Templar of Oklahoma, *Proceedings of the 66th Annual Conclave* (Oklahoma: 1961).

[6] Grand Commandery of Knights Templar of Oklahoma, *Proceedings of the 67th Annual Conclave* (Oklahoma: 1962).

[7] Grand Commandery of Knights Templar of Oklahoma, *Proceedings of the 91st Annual Conclave* (Oklahoma: 1986).

[8] Grand Commandery of Knights Templar of Oklahoma, *Proceedings of the 69th Annual Conclave* (Oklahoma: 1964).

[9] Grand Commandery of Knights Templar of Oklahoma, *Proceedings of the 71st Annual Conclave* (Oklahoma: 1966).

[10] Grand Commandery of Knights Templar of Oklahoma, *Proceedings of the 77th Annual Conclave* (Oklahoma: 1972).

[11] Grand Commandery of Knights Templar of Oklahoma, *Proceedings of the 70th Annual Conclave* (Oklahoma: 1965).

[12] Grand Commandery of Knights Templar of Oklahoma, *Proceedings of the 75th Annual Conclave* (Oklahoma: 1970).

[13] Grand Commandery of Knights Templar of Oklahoma, *Proceedings of the 83rd Annual Conclave* (Oklahoma: 1978).

[14] Grand Commandery of Knights Templar of Oklahoma, *Proceedings of the 84th Annual Conclave*.

[15] Grand Commandery of Knights Templar of Oklahoma, *Proceedings of the 94th Annual Conclave* (Oklahoma: 1989).

[16] "Area Assignments," Oklahoma York Rite, <http://okyorkrite.org/contact-us.htm>, Accessed 4 July 2012.

[17] "Past Department Commanders," The Grand Encampment of Knights Templar, <http://www.knightstemplar.org/pgeo/pdc.html>, Accessed 4 July 2012.

[18] Grand Commandery of Knights Templar of Oklahoma, *Proceedings of the 66th Annual Conclave*.

[19] Grand Commandery of Knights Templar of Oklahoma, *Proceedings of the 67th Annual Conclave*.

[20] "Past Department Commanders."

[21] "Past Grand Prelates," The Grand Encampment of Knights Templar, <http://www.knightstemplar.org/pgeo/gp.html>, Accessed 4 July 2012.

[22] Grand Commandery of Knights Templar of Oklahoma, *Proceedings of the 116th Annual Conclave* (Oklahoma: 2011).

[23] Grand Commandery of Knights Templar of Oklahoma, *Proceedings of the 77th Annual Conclave*.

[24] Grand Commandery of Knights Templar of Oklahoma, *Proceedings of the 81st Annual Conclave* (Oklahoma: 1976).

[25] Grand Commandery of Knights Templar of Oklahoma, *Proceedings of the 95th Annual Conclave* (Oklahoma: 1990).

[26] Grand Commandery of Knights Templar of Oklahoma, *Proceedings of the 71st Annual Conclave*.

[27] Grand Commandery of Knights Templar of Oklahoma, *Proceedings of the 72nd Annual Conclave* (Oklahoma: 1967).

[28] Grand Commandery of Knights Templar of Oklahoma, *Proceedings of the 82nd Annual Conclave* (Oklahoma: 1977).

[29] Ibid.

[30] Grand Commandery of Knights Templar of Oklahoma, *Proceedings of the 101st Annual Conclave* (Oklahoma: 1996).

[31] Grand Commandery of Knights Templar of Oklahoma, *Proceedings of the 92nd Annual Conclave* (Oklahoma: 1987).

[32] Grand Commandery of Knights Templar of Oklahoma, *Proceedings of the 93rd Annual Conclave* (Oklahoma: 1988).

[33] Grand Commandery of Knights Templar of Oklahoma, *Proceedings of the 103rd Annual Conclave* (Oklahoma: 1998).

[34] Grand Commandery of Knights Templar of Oklahoma, *Proceedings of the 105th Annual Conclave* (Oklahoma: 2000).

[35] Grand Commandery of Knights Templar of Oklahoma, *Proceedings of the 108th Annual Conclave* (Oklahoma: 2003).

[36] Grand Commandery of Knights Templar of Oklahoma, *Proceedings of the 71st Annual Conclave*.

[37] Grand Commandery of Knights Templar of Oklahoma, *Proceedings of the 114th Annual Conclave* (Oklahoma: 2009).

[38] Grand Commandery of Knights Templar of Oklahoma, *Proceedings of the 115th Annual Conclave* (Oklahoma: 2010).

[39] Grand Commandery of Knights Templar of Oklahoma, *Proceedings of the 117th Annual Conclave* (Oklahoma: 2012).

[40] Grand Commandery of Knights Templar of Oklahoma, *Proceedings of the 77th Annual Conclave*.

[41] Grand Commandery of Knights Templar of Oklahoma, *Proceedings of the 76th Annual Conclave* (Oklahoma: 1971).

[42] Grand Commandery of Knights Templar of Oklahoma, *Proceedings of the 63rd Annual Conclave* (Oklahoma: 1958).

[43] "Cameron University," Oklahoma Historical Society's Encyclopedia of Oklahoma History and Culture, <http://digital.library.okstate.edu/encyclopedia/entries/C/CA019.html>, Accessed 6 July 2012.

[44] Grand Commandery of Knights Templar of Oklahoma, *Proceedings of the 104th Annual Conclave* (Oklahoma: 1999).

[45] Grand Commandery of Knights Templar of Oklahoma, *Proceedings of the 117th Annual Conclave*.

[46] Grand Commandery of Knights Templar of Oklahoma, *Proceedings of the 78th Annual Conclave* (Oklahoma: 1973).

[47] Grand Commandery of Knights Templar of Oklahoma, *Proceedings of the 82nd Annual Conclave*.

[48] Grand Commandery of Knights Templar of Oklahoma, *Proceedings of the 87th Annual Conclave* (Oklahoma: 1982).

[49] Grand Commandery of Knights Templar of Oklahoma, *Proceedings of the 99th Annual*

Conclave (Oklahoma: 1994).

[50] Grand Commandery of Knights Templar of Oklahoma, *Proceedings of the 103rd Annual Conclave* (Oklahoma: 1998).

[51] "History," Masonic Charity Foundation of Oklahoma, <http://www.mcfok.org/about/history/>, Accessed 6 July 2012.

[52] Grand Commandery of Knights Templar of Oklahoma, *Proceedings of the 91st Annual Conclave* (Oklahoma: 1986).

[53] Grand Commandery of Knights Templar of Oklahoma, *Proceedings of the 92nd Annual Conclave*.

[54] Grand Commandery of Knights Templar of Oklahoma, *Proceedings of the 93rd Annual Conclave*.

[55] Grand Commandery of Knights Templar of Oklahoma, *Proceedings of the 107th Annual Conclave* (Oklahoma: 2002).

[56] "2012 Officers & Board," Masonic Charity Foundation of Oklahoma, <http://www.mcfok.org/about/officers-and-board/>, Accessed 6 July 2012.

[57] Grand Commandery of Knights Templar of Oklahoma, *Proceedings of the 102nd Annual Conclave* (Oklahoma: 1997).

[58] "The York Rite of Freemasonry, its Appendant Bodies, and Other Allied Masonic Organizatons," York Rite Freemasonry Official Information Site, <http://www.yorkrite.com/degrees/>, Accessed 6 July 2012.

[59] Stephen Dafoe, *Morgan: The The Scandal That Shook Freemasonry* (New Orleans: Cornerstone Book Publishers, 2009), 138.

[60] "Past Grand Masters from 1816," The Grand Encampment of Knights Templar, <http://www.knightstemplar.org/pgeo/mepgm.html>, Accessed 6 July 2012.

[61] Robert G. Davis, General Secretary, Guthrie Scottish Rite, Interview, June 11, 2012.

[62] Grand Commandery of Knights Templar of Oklahoma, *Proceedings of the 116th Annual Conclave*.

[63] Robert G. Davis and Frank A. Derr, *100 Years of Scottish Rite Masonry in the Valley of Guthrie* (Oklahoma: Guthrie Valley AASR), 31.

[64] Davis.

[65] Grand Commandery of Knights Templar of Oklahoma, *Proceedings of the 104th Annual Conclave* (Oklahoma: 1999).

[66] Grand Commandery of Knights Templar of Oklahoma, *Proceedings of the 105th Annual Conclave*.

[67] Grand Commandery of Knights Templar of Oklahoma, *Proceedings of the 106th Annual Conclave* (Oklahoma: 2001).

[68] Grand Commandery of Knights Templar of Oklahoma, *Proceedings of the 103rd Annual Conclave*.

[69] Grand Commandery of Knights Templar of Oklahoma, *Proceedings of the 111th Annual Conclave* (Oklahoma: 2006).

[70] Davis.

[71] Barbara Frale, *The Templars: The Secret History Revealed* (New York: Arcade Publishing, 2009).

[72] Davis.

[73] Grand Commandery of Knights Templar of Oklahoma, *Proceedings of the 113th Annual Conclave* (Oklahoma: 2008).

[74] Grand Commandery of Knights Templar of Oklahoma, *Proceedings of the 115th Annual Conclave*.

[75] Grand Commandery of Knights Templar of Oklahoma, *Proceedings of the 116th Annual Conclave*.

[76] Grand Commandery of Knights Templar of Oklahoma, *Proceedings of the 117th Annual Conclave*.

[77] Grand Commandery of Knights Templar of Oklahoma, *Proceedings of the 116th Annual Conclave*.

[78] "Prince Hall Masonry Recognition Details," Paul M. Bessel, <http://bessel.org/masrec/phaugle.htm>, Accessed 8 July 2012.

[79] Grand Commandery of Knights Templar of Oklahoma, *Proceedings of the 115th Annual Conclave*.

[80] Grand Commandery of Knights Templar of Oklahoma, *Proceedings of the 117th Annual Conclave*.

[81] Grand Commandery of Knights Templar of Oklahoma, *Proceedings of the 115th Annual Conclave*.

Appendix A

Commanderies Chartered

Grand Commandery of the Indian Territory
Chartered December 27, 1895

Muskogee No. 1	August 11, 1892	Muskogee
Chickasaw No. 2	August 29, 1895	Purcell
McAlester No. 3	August 29, 1895	McAlester
DeMolay No. 4	August 10, 1896	Chickasha
Ardmore No. 5	November 2, 1897	Ardmore
Ada No. 6	April 22, 1905	Ada
Trinity No. 7	April 19, 1906	Tulsa
Gethsemane No. 8	April 23, 1908	Okmulgee
Calvary No. 9	April 23, 1908	Bartlesville
Okemah No. 10	April 23, 1909	Okemah
Hugo No. 11	April 22, 1910	Hugo
Durant No. 12	April 22, 1910	Durant
Hugh de Payen No. 13	April 22, 1910	Atoka
Sapulpa No. 14	April 22, 1910	Sapulpa

Grand Commandery of Oklahoma
Chartered February 10, 1896

Guthrie No. 1	August 11, 1892	Guthrie
Oklahoma No. 2	August 11, 1892	Oklahoma City
Ascension No. 3	August 29, 1895	El Reno
St. Johns No. 4	February 1, 1897	Stillwater
Perry No. 5	April 10, 1900	Perry
Cyrene No. 6	April 10, 1901	Kingfisher
Pawnee No. 7	April 10, 1901	Pawnee
Enid No. 8	February 14, 1902	Enid
Ben Hur No. 9	February 12, 1903	Ponca City
Hobart No. 10	February 16, 1905	Hobart
Weatherford No. 11	February 15, 1906	Weatherford
Lawton No. 12	February 15, 1906	Lawton
Frederick No. 13	February 15, 1906	Frederick
Ivanhoe No. 14	March 20, 1907	Sayre

Elk City No. 15	March 20, 1907	Elk City
Emanuel No. 16	March 20, 1907	Blackwell
Lincoln No. 17	March 20, 1907	Chandler
Eldorado No. 18	February 16, 1909	Eldorado
St. Aumer No. 19	March 8, 1910	Taloga
Foraker No. 20	February 21, 1911	Foraker
Palestine No. 21	February 21, 1911	Pawhuska

Grand Commandery of Oklahoma
Consolidated October 6, 1911

Guthrie No. 1	July 12, 1890(d)	Guthrie
Muskogee No. 2	October 1, 1891(d)	Muskogee
Oklahoma No. 3	March 5, 1892(d)	Oklahoma City
Ascension No. 4	May 8, 1893(d)	El Reno
Chickasaw No. 5	May 31, 1894(d)	Purcell
McAlester No. 6	July 14, 1894(d)	McAlester
DeMolay No. 7	August 19, 1896	Chickasha
St. Johns No. 8	February 1, 1897	Stillwater
Ardmore No. 9	November 2, 1897	Ardmore
Perry No. 10	April 10, 1900	Perry
Cyrene No. 11	April 10, 1901	Kingfisher
Pawnee No. 12	April 10, 1901	Pawnee
Enid No. 13	February 14, 1902	Enid
Ben Hur No. 14	February 12, 1903	Ponca City
Hobart No. 15	February 16, 1905	Hobart
Ada No. 16	April 22, 1905	Ada
Weatherford No. 17	February 15, 1906	Weatherford
Lawton No. 18	February 15, 1906	Lawton
Frederick No. 19	February 15, 1906	Frederick
Trinity No. 20	April 19, 1906	Tulsa
Ivanhoe No. 21	March 20, 1907	Sayre
Elk City No. 22	March 20, 1907	Elk City
Emmanuel No. 23	March 20, 1907	Blackwell

Lincoln No. 24	March 20, 1907	Chandler
Gethsemane No. 25	April 23, 1908	Okmulgee
Calvary No. 26	April 23, 1908	Bartlesville
Eldorado No. 27	February 16, 1909	Eldorado
Okemah No. 28	April 23, 1909	Okemah
St. Aumer No. 29	March 8, 1910	Taloga
Hugo No. 30	April 22, 1910	Hugo
Durant No. 31	April 22, 1910	Durant
Hugh de Payen No. 32	April 22, 1910	Atoka
Sapulpa No. 33	April 22, 1910	Sapulpa
Foraker No. 34	February 21, 1911	Foraker
Palestine No. 35	February 21, 1911	Pawhuska
Shawnee No. 36	April 19, 1912	Shawnee
St. Augustine No. 37	April 19, 1912	Alva
Norman No. 38	April 24, 1914	Norman
Malta No. 39	April 21, 1916	Heavener
Poteau No. 40	April 21, 1916	Poteau
Claremore No. 41	April 21, 1916	Claremore
Cushing No. 42	April 17, 1919	Cushing
Holdenville No. 43	May 17, 1922	Holdenville
Cleveland No. 44	May 17, 1922	Cleveland
Bethlehem No. 45	May 17, 1922	Oklahoma City
Duncan No. 46	May 23, 1923	Duncan
Drumright No. 47	May 21, 1924	Drumright
Hominy No. 48	May 20, 1925	Hominy
Miami No. 49	May 18, 1927	Miami
Hugh de Payen No. 50	April 26, 1960	Atoka
Guymon No. 51	April 25, 1961	Guymon
Tipton No. 52	May 8, 1989	Tipton
Capitol Hill No. 53	May 8, 1989	Oklahoma City

(d) – date of dispensation

Grand Commandery of Oklahoma
Active as of 2012

Guthrie No. 1	August 11, 1892	Guthrie
Muskogee No. 2	August 11, 1892	Muskogee
Oklahoma No. 3	August 11, 1892	Oklahoma City
McAlester No. 6	August 29, 1895	McAlester
St. Johns No. 8	February 1, 1897	Stillwater
Ardmore No. 9	November 2, 1897	Ardmore
Ben Hur No. 14	February 12, 1903	Ponca City
Lawton No. 18	February 15, 1906	Lawton
Trinity No. 20	April 19, 1906	Tulsa
Elk City No. 22	March 20, 1907	Elk City
Gethsemane No. 25	April 23, 1908	Okmulgee
Calvary No. 26	April 23, 1908	Bartlesville
St. Aumer No. 29	March 8, 1910	Woodward
Norman No. 38	April 24, 1914	Norman
Cimarron Valley No. 42	April 17, 1919	Drumright
Capitol Hill No. 53	May 8, 1989	Midwest City

Appendix B

Grand Commander Portraits

Grand Commandery of the Indian Territory

Robert W. Hill
1895-1896

James E. Humphrey
1896-1897

Edmond H. Doyle
1897-1898

Patrick J. Byrne
1898-1899

Ira B. Kirkland
1900-1901

Zachary T. Walrond
1901-1902

Daniel M. Hailey
1902-1903

Herbert J. Evans
1903-1904

John Coyle
1905-1906

Frank Smith
1906-1907

James Elliott
1907-1908

John W. Speake
1908-1909

Christopher Springer
1909-1910

Roy D. Fuller
1910-1911

Grand Commandery of Oklahoma

Cassius M. Barnes
1896-1897

DeForest F. Leach
1897-1898

Otto A. Shuttee
1898-1899

William S. Spencer
1899-1900

Harper S. Cunningham
1900-1901

Julius C. Cross
1901-1902

Henry E. Hand
1902-1903

Enoch M. Bamford
1903-1904

C.A. Morris
1904-1905

William J. Pettee
1905-1906

Charles P. Wickmiller
1906-1907

Henry K. Ricker
1907-1908

William L. Eagleton
1908-1909

John C. Flemming
1909-1910

Edward P. Gallup
1910-1911

John R. Hamill
1911

Robert H. Henry
1911-1912

Guy W. Bohannan
1912-1913

William H. Essex
1913-1914

J. Angus Gillis
1914-1915

James A. Scott
1915-1916

James Q. Louthan
1916-1917

Eugene P. McMahon
1917-1918

Charles S. Highsmith
1918-1919

Fred H. Clark
1919-1920

Milton C. Hale
1920-1921

Harold B. Downing
1921-1922

Orin Ashton
1922-1923

W. Clark Tucker
1923-1924

Charles W. Tedrowe
1924-1925

Sydnor H. Lester
1925-1926

William R. Lence
1926-1927

Bert D. Ashbrook
1927-1928

James C. Johnson
1928-1929

Leslie H. Swan
1929-1930

Ralph V. Downing
1930-1931

Gilbert Presnell
1931-1932

Emerson Burns
1932-1933

Walter M. Rainey
1933-1934

Robert H. Phinney
1934-1935

Layton S. Chilcutt
1935-1936

Harold G. Durnell
1936-1937

Merl P. Long
1937-1938

Richard E. Newhouse
1938-1939

John I. Taylor
1939-1940

William E. Crowe
1940-1941

Ernest C. Lambert
1941-1942

Harry M. House
1942-1943

Hal F. Rambo
1943-1944

Marvin A. Wilson
1944-1945

John J. Moffatt
1945-1946

Victor G. Heller
1946-1947

Wilbur P. Lee
1947-1948

Paul O. Creason
1948-1949

Leonard A. Maphet
1949-1950

William H. King
1950-1951

Glenn B. Young
1951-1952

Charles C. Lynch
1952-1953

Clell C. Warriner
1953-1954

Ansel M. Crowder
1954-1955

Rennie L. Moore
1955-1956

George E. Schutz
1956-1957

Oliver S. Willham
1957-1958

Walter R. Pearson
1958-1959

J. Milton McCullough
1959-1960

Carl F. Hansen
1960-1961

Ernest T. Ross
1961-1962

Irvin Cecil
1962-1963

Robert W. Rogers
1963-1964

Richard B. Burch
1964-1965

Paul W. Alexander
1965-1966

Frederick J. Smith
1966-1967

James J. Thorne
1967-1968

Willis H. Gorey
1968-1969

Clyde S. Heckrodt
1969-1970

August S. Johnson
1970-1971

Jack Freeman
1971-1972

C.W. Reese
1972-1973

James C. Abernathy
1973-1974

James C. Taylor
1974-1975

Walter L. Harmon

1975-1976

Odie E. Earnest

1976-1977

Norman P. Bullock
1977-1978

Otis K. Taylor
1978-1979

Herbert A. Skillings
1979-1980

Robert L. Taylor
1980-1981

Donald J. Cink
1981-1982

John C. Shanklin
1982-1983

Lilburn M. Pierce
1983-1984

Ellis Sappington
1984-1985

Darrel W. Hughes
1985-1986

Joe S. Warriner
1986-1987

Leon A. Anderson
1987-1988

Daniel C. Pryor
1988-1989

Kenneth D. Buckley
1989-1990

Eugene Smith
1990-1991

Bartis M. Kent
1991-1992

Calvin E. Mettee
1992-1993

Rex L. Eutsler
1993-1994

Don L. Turley
1994-1995

James R. Creason
1995-1996

William A. "Pete" Nation
1996-1997

Edward W. Hart
1997-1998

O. Ray Harrington
1998-1999

Jon J. Giddings
1999-2000

Charles L. Stuckey
2000-2001

John A. Schrawger, Jr.
2001-2002

William H. Pierce
2002-2003

Glenn H. Kinsley
2003-2004

Gary A. Davis
2004-2005

Robert G. Davis
2005-2006

Willis L. Emerson
2006-2007

John L. Logan
2007-2008

Michael E. Hampton
2008-2009

Lewis A. Hullum
2009-2010

I. Dwayne Dixon
2010-2011

Richard C. Dunaway
2011-2012

Mark A. Critchfield
2012-2013

Appendix C

Past Grand Officers

Grand Commandery of the Indian Territory

	Grand Commander	Grand Treasurer	Grand Recorder
1895	Robert W. Hill	J. J. McAlester	Leo Bennett
1896	James E. Humphrey	J. J. McAlester	Leo Bennett
1897	Edmond H. Doyle	G. H. Williams	Joseph S. Murrow
1898	Patrick J. Byrne	G. H. Williams	Joseph S. Murrow
1899	Robert F. Scoffern	G. H. Williams	Joseph S. Murrow
1900	Ira B. Kirkland	G. H. Williams	Joseph S. Murrow
1901	Z. T. Walrond	H. L. Jarboe, Jr.	Joseph S. Murrow
1902	Daniel M. Hailey	Ira B. Kirkland	Joseph S. Murrow
1903	Herbert J. Evans	Ira B. Kirkland	Joseph S. Murrow
1904	William F. Bowman	Ira B. Kirkland	Joseph S. Murrow
1905	John Coyle	Ira B. Kirkland	Joseph S. Murrow
1906	Frank Smith	Ira B. Kirkland	Joseph S. Murrow
1907	James Elliott	Ira B. Kirkland	Joseph S. Murrow
1908	John W. Speak	Ira B. Kirkland	Joseph S. Murrow
1909	Christ. Springer	Ira B. Kirkland	Edmond H. Doyle
1910	Roy D. Fuller	Ira B. Kirkland	Edmond H. Doyle
1911	Ira McNair	Ira B. Kirkland	Eugene Hamilton

Grand Commandery of Oklahoma

	Grand Commander	Grand Treasurer	Grand Recorder
1896	C.M. Barnes	Luke Ellison	H. S. Cunningham
1897	DeDorest D. Leach	Luke Ellison	H. S. Cunningham
1898	Otto A. Shuttee	Luke Ellison	H. S. Cunningham
1899	W. S. Spencer	Luke Ellison	DeDorest D. Leach
1900	H. S. Cunningham	Luke Ellison	DeDorest D. Leach
1901	Julius C. Cross	Luke Ellison	DeDorest D. Leach
1902	Henry E. Hand	W. S. Spencer	H. S. Cunningham
1903	Enoch M. Bamford	W. S. Spencer	H. S. Cunningham
1904	C. A. Morris	W. S. Spencer	H. S. Cunningham
1905	W. J. Pettee	Otto A. Shuttee	George W. Spencer
1906	C. P. Wickmiller	Otto A. Shuttee	George W. Spencer
1907	Henry K. Ricker	Otto A. Shuttee	George W. Spencer
1908	W. L. Eagleton	Otto A. Shuttee	George W. Spencer
1909	John C. Fleming	Otto A. Shuttee	George W. Spencer
1910	Edward P. Gallup	Otto A. Shuttee	George W. Spencer
1911	John R. Hamill	Otto A. Shuttee	George W. Spencer
1911	Robert H. Henry	Ira B. Kirkland	George W. Spencer

1912	Guy W. Bohannon	Ira B. Kirkland	George W. Spencer
1913	William H. Essex	Ira B. Kirkland	George W. Spencer
1914	J. Angus Gillis	Ira B. Kirkland	George W. Spencer
1915	James A. Scott	Ira B. Kirkland	George W. Spencer
1916	James Q. Louthan	Ira B. Kirkland	George W. Spencer
1917	Eugene P. McMahon	Ira B. Kirkland	George W. Spencer
1918	C. S. Highsmith	Ira B. Kirkland	George W. Spencer
1919	Fred H. Clark	Ira B. Kirkland	George W. Spencer
1920	Milton C. Hale	Ira B. Kirkland	George W. Spencer
1921	Harold B. Downing	Ira B. Kirkland	George W. Spencer
1922	Orin Ashton	Ira B. Kirkland	George W. Spencer
1923	W. Clark Tucker	Ira B. Kirkland	George W. Spencer
1924	C. W. Tedrowe	Ira B. Kirkland	George W. Spencer
1925	Sydnor H. Lester	Ira B. Kirkland	George W. Spencer
1926	W. R. Lence	Ira B. Kirkland	George W. Spencer
1927	Bert D. Ashbrook	Ira B. Kirkland	George W. Spencer
1928	James C. Johnson	Ira B. Kirkland	George W. Spencer
1929	Leslie H. Swan	Ira B. Kirkland	George W. Spencer
1930	Ralph V. Downing	Ira B. Kirkland	George W. Spencer
1931	Gilbert Presnell	Ira B. Kirkland	George W. Spencer
1932	E. Burns	Ira B. Kirkland	George W. Spencer
1933	Walter M. Rainey	Ira B. Kirkland	George W. Spencer
1934	R. H. Phinney	Ira B. Kirkland	J. A. Latham
1935	Layton S. Chilcutt	Ralph V. Downing	J. A. Latham
1936	Harold G. Durnell	W. Clark Tucker	J. A. Latham
1937	Merl P. Long	W. Clark Tucker	J. A. Latham
1938	R. E. Newhouse	W. Clark Tucker	J. A. Latham
1939	John I. Taylor	W. Clark Tucker	J. A. Latham
1940	W. E. Crowe	W. Clark Tucker	J. A. Latham
1941	E. C. Lambert	W. Clark Tucker	J. A. Latham
1942	Harry M. House	W. Clark Tucker	J. A. Latham
1943	Hal F. Rambo	W. Clark Tucker	J. A. Latham
1944	Marvin A. Wilson	W. Clark Tucker	J. A. Latham
1945	John J. Moffatt	W. Clark Tucker	J. A. Latham
1946	V. G. Heller	W. Clark Tucker	J. A. Latham
1947	Wilbur P. Lee	Ralph L. Dunkle	J. A. Latham
1948	P. O. Creason	Ralph L. Dunkle	J. A. Latham
1949	L. A. Maphet	Ralph L. Dunkle	J. A. Latham
1950	W. H. King	Ralph L. Dunkle	J. A. Latham
1951	G. B. Young	Ralph L. Dunkle	J. A. Latham

1952	C. C. Lynch	Ralph L. Dunkle	J. A. Latham
1953	C. C. Warriner	Ralph L. Dunkle	J. A. Latham
1954	A. M. Crowder	Ralph L. Dunkle	J. A. Latham
1955	R. L. Moore	Ralph L. Dunkle	J. A. Latham
1956	G. E. Schutz	W. H. King	J. A. Latham
1957	O. S. Willham	W. H. King	J. A. Latham
1958	W. R. Pearson	W. H. King	J. A. Latham
1959	J. M. McCullough	W. H. King	J. A. Latham
1960	C. F. Hansen	W. H. King	J. A. Latham
1961	Ernest T. Ross	W. H. King	J. A. Latham
1962	Irvin Cecil	W. H. King	J. A. Latham
1963	R. W. Rogers	W. H. King	F. M. Lumbard
1964	R. D. Burch	W. H. King	F. M. Lumbard
1965	P. W. Alexander	W. H. King	F. M. Lumbard
1966	F. J. Smith	W. H. King	F. M. Lumbard
1967	J. J. Thorne	W. H. King	F. M. Lumbard
1968	W. H. Gorey	W. H. King	F. M. Lumbard
1969	C. S. Heckrodt	W. H. King	F. M. Lumbard
1970	A. S. Johnson	W. H. King	F. M. Lumbard
1971	Jack Freeman	W. H. King	F. M. Lumbard
1972	C. W. Reese	W. H. King	F. M. Lumbard
1973	J. C. Abernathy	A. S. Johnson	F. M. Lumbard
1974	James C. Taylor	A. S. Johnson	F. M. Lumbard
1975	Walter L. Harmon	A. S. Johnson	F. M. Lumbard
1976	Odie E. Earnest	A. S. Johnson	F. M. Lumbard
1977	Norman P. Bullock	J. C. Abernathy	F. M. Lumbard
1978	O. Kenneth Taylor	J. C. Abernathy	F. M. Lumbard
1979	H. A. Skillings	J. C. Abernathy	F. M. Lumbard
1980	Robert L. Taylor	J. C. Abernathy	F. M. Lumbard
1981	Donald J. Cink	J. C. Abernathy	Robert E. Fielden
1982	John C. Shanklin	J. C. Abernathy	Robert E. Fielden
1983	Lilburn Pearce	J. C. Abernathy	Robert E. Fielden
1984	Ellis Sappington	J. C. Abernathy	Donald J. Cink
1985	Darrel W. Hughes	J. C. Abernathy	Donald J. Cink
1986	Joe S. Warriner	J. C. Abernathy	Donald J. Cink
1987	Leon A. Anderson	J. C. Abernathy	Donald J. Cink
1988	Daniel C. Pryor	J. C. Abernathy	Donald J. Cink
1989	Kenneth D. Buckley	J. C. Abernathy	Donald J. Cink
1990	Eugene Smith	J. C. Abernathy	Donald J. Cink
1991	Bartis M. Kent	J. C. Abernathy	Donald J. Cink

1992	Calvin E. Mettee	J. C. Abernathy	Donald J. Cink
1993	Rex L. Eutsler	J. C. Abernathy	Donald J. Cink
1994	Don L. Turley	Kish L. Thomas	Donald J. Cink
1995	James R. Creason	Kish L. Thomas	Donald J. Cink
1996	William A. Nation	Kish L. Thomas	Donald J. Cink
1997	Edward W. Hart	Kish L. Thomas	Don H. Haralson
1998	O. Ray Harrington	Kish L. Thomas	David A. Ray
1999	Jon J. Giddings	Kish L. Thomas	Ralph K. Harris
2000	Charles L. Stuckey	Kish L. Thomas	Ralph K. Harris
2001	John A. Schrawger	Kish L. Thomas	Ralph K. Harris
2002	William H. Pierce	Kish L. Thomas	John D. Miller, Jr.
2003	Glenn H. Kinsley	Kish L. Thomas	John D. Miller, Jr.
2004	Gary A. Davis	Elwood M. Isaacs	John D. Miller, Jr.
2005	Robert G. Davis	Elwood M. Isaacs	Gary A. Davis
2006	Willis L. Emerson	Elwood M. Isaacs	Gary A. Davis
2007	John L. Logan	Elwood M. Isaacs	Gary A. Davis
2008	Michael E. Hampton	Elwood M. Isaacs	Gary A. Davis
2009	Lewis A. Hullum	Elwood M. Isaacs	Gary A. Davis
2010	I. Dwayne Dixon	Elwood M. Isaacs	Gary A. Davis
2011	Richard C. Dunaway	Elwood M. Isaacs	Gary A. Davis
2012	Mark A. Critchfield	Elwood M. Isaacs	Gary A. Davis

Appendix D

Knights Templar Cross of Honor

The Knights Templar Cross of Honor was created at the 49th Triennial of the Grand Encampment of the United States of America held a Philadelphia in 1964. From General Order No. 5 of the Grand Encampment:

> The Knights Templar Cross of Honor shall be awarded for exceptional and meritorious service rendered to the Order of Knights Templar, far beyond the call of duty, and beyond the service usually expected of an Officer or Member. Only one nomination for such award may be made by a Grand Commander from among the Sir Knights of his Grand Commandery during any one year.[1]

Recipients of the Knights Templar Cross of Honor

1965 – Alfred S. Bryan, DeMolay Commandery No. 7, Chickasha
1967 – Olin V. Homes, Muskogee Commandery No. 2, Muskogee
1968 – William A. Perry, Gethsemane Commandery No. 25, Okmulgee
1969 – Ivan Saye, Trinity Commandery No. 20, Tulsa
1970 – Leroy Hudson, Miami Commandery No. 49, Miami
1971 – G. T. Hayes, Elk City Commandery No. 22, Elk City
1972 – Myrl S. Kirk, Enid Commandery No. 13, Enid
1973 – Chester L. Moffett, Shawnee Commandery No. 36, Shawnee
1974 – Everett Carbaugh, Bethlehem Commandery No. 45, Oklahoma City
1975 – Edwin A. Lane, Ben Hur Commandery No. 14, Ponca City
1976 – Dennis H. Clay, Cushing Commandery No. 42, Cushing
1977 – Ralph L. Barnhart, Gethsemane Commandery No. 25, Okmulgee
1978 – Robert H. Bibb, Muskogee Commandery No. 2, Muskogee
1979 – Russell L. Maxwell, Trinity Commandery No. 20, Tulsa

---

[1] Grand Commandery of Knights Templar of Oklahoma, *Proceedings of the 70th Annual Conclave* (Oklahoma: 1965).

1980 – Allan J. Larson, Ardmore Commandery No. 9, Ardmore
1981 – Joseph S. Lewis, Ben Hur Commandery No. 14, Ponca City
1982 – Henry J. Berline, Emmanuel Commandery No. 23. Blackwell
1983 – A. B. Harrison, St. John's Commandery No. 8, Stillwater
1984 – Guy Bowman, Enid Commandery No. 13, Enid
1985 – William McBride, Trinity Commandery No. 20, Tulsa
1986 – L. D. Clark, Oklahoma Commandery No. 3, Oklahoma City
1987 – Chester M. Cowen, DeMolay Commandery No. 7, Chickasha
1988 – Melvin M. Jennings, Lawton Commandery No. 18, Lawton
1989 – Charles J. Engle, Bartlesville Commandery No. 26, Bartlesville
1990 – Kurt Schutz, Lawton Commandery No. 18, Lawton
1991 – Robert E. Goode, Bartlesville Commandery No. 26, Bartlesville
1992 – Andrew J. Vloedman, St. Aumer Commandery No. 29, Woodward
1993 – William L. Keeling, Muskogee Commandery No. 2, Muskogee
1994 – Donald W. Rimmer, Norman Commandery No. 38, Norman
1995 – Carl R. Burrows, Lawton Commandery No. 18, Lawton
1996 – Frederick S. Sloan, Elk City Commandery No. 22, Elk City
1997 – James H. Lasley, Ardmore Commandery No. 9, Ardmore
1998 – Forrest T. Smith, Guthrie Commandery No. 1, Guthrie
1999 – Earl J. Berryman, Jr., Oklahoma No. 3, Oklahoma City
2000 – James E. Smyrl, Trinity No. 20, Tulsa
2001 – Gene D. Harper, Ardmore No. 9, Ardmore
2002 – Robert T. Shipe, Capitol Hill Commandery No. 53, Midwest City
2004 – William W. Williams, Guthrie Commandery No. 1, Guthrie
2005 – Hollis O. Edgar, Cimarron Valley Commandery No. 42, Drumright
2006 – Edwin C. Womack, Elk City Commandery No. 22, Elk City
2007 – Paul T. Currell, Elk City Commandery No. 22, Elk City
2008 – Timothy P. Israel, Elk City Commandery No. 22, Elk City
2009 – Matthew McGee, Ben Hur Commandery No. 14, Ponca City
2010 – Trasen S. Akers, Norman Commandery No. 38, Norman
2011 – Alfred D. Fryman, Jr., Elk City Commandery No. 22, Elk City
2012 – James N. Rossi, Capitol Hill Commandery No. 53, Midwest City

Appendix D

Masonic Papers of Note

Templar Treasures
By Trasen S. Akers

Many Masonic Bodies across the United States have come into possession of various treasures over the years. These can range from simple minute books from bygone eras that bear the signatures of important men of the times to more awe inspiring items. For example, Norman Masonic Lodge No. 38 AF&AM proudly displays a tyler's register from 1899 bearing the signature of James S. Buchanan who was the fourth President of the University of Oklahoma.[1] It is in the antechamber of Lawton Commandery No. 18 in Lawton, Oklahoma that a truly great Templar treasure can be found.

Old cannoneers will know the city of Lawton as being adjacent to Fort Sill which was constructed in 1869 by elements of the 10th US Cavalry and the 6th US Infantry. Eventually the School of Fire was established at Fort Sill in 1911.[2] Fort Sill and the military in general have long had a connection with the Fraternity in Oklahoma. In December of 1917, over two-hundred soldiers from Camp Doniphan at Ft. Sill were given passes to journey to Guthrie for a special Scottish Rite reunion; it was the first time Oklahoma Consistory No. 1 conferred all 29 degrees and with a class composed entirely of servicemen. Due to the number of soldiers interested in being made 32° Masons, the post commander issued an order limiting the number of passes that could be issued at any one time. With this restriction on the number of troops that could leave the post, the Guthrie Scottish Rite Bodies erected a Masonic "club house" on site for the purpose of communicating the degrees on soldiers. Even Harry Truman, then a Lieutenant, is on record as having visited the Guthrie Valley AASR during this time.[3] In addition to this

Masonic activity, the Fort Sill Masonic Club long had a presence on the post and could count men such a Brigadier General Dwight E. Aultman, a former post commander, among its members.[4]

General Aultman certainly was not the only general officer associated with the Masonic Fraternity in Oklahoma though. Throughout its history a number of generals of the Oklahoma National Guard have been Masons. General Ewell L. Head of Muskogee served with the Guard prior to WWII and was an active member of both the Bedouin Shrine and the Knights Templar.[5] General Hal L. Muldrow of Norman, the son of the first Grand Master of the State of Oklahoma, was a member of the McAlester Valley AASR. Generals William S. Key of Seminole and Frederick A. Daugherty of Oklahoma City both held the post of Sovereign Grand Inspector General in Oklahoma.[6]

It was in the late 1940s that an artillery officer stationed at Fort Sill, Major Ralph L. Paddock Jr., presented a special gift to the Sir Knights of Lawton.[7] As one enters the asylum they will notice a large shadow box hanging in the antechamber that contains what appears to be a rather non-descript sword of Nebraska regulation, some letters, a photo, and two brass plaques. Upon closer inspection the curious will find that this particular sword bears the name of one of this Nation's great military heroes, General John J. Pershing. It is only fitting that such a memento would be deposited in a locale steeped in Military History.

Pershing was born in Missouri in 1860 and had the privilege of growing up in an era of some of America's greatest generals.[8] He graduated from the United States Military Academy in 1886, where his classmates recognized that he possessed a rare quality of leadership. Upon graduation, Pershing was assigned to the 6th US Cavalry and sent to Fort Bayard, NM. In 1891 he reported to the University of Nebraska to serve as Professor of Military Science and Tactics.[9] Pershing had previously taken the degrees of Freemasonry in December of 1888 in Lincoln Lodge No. 19 of Lincoln, Nebraska. It was while posted at the University of Nebraska that he was exalted in Lincoln Chapter No. 6 on March 28, 1894 and was dubbed and created a Knight of the Temple on Dec. 3, 1894 in Mt. Moriah Commandery No. 4.[10]

Knights Templar Sword of General John J. Pershing
Courtesy of T.S. Akers

After serving in Cuba in 1898, Pershing left for Manilla to fight the Moros. It was while in Cuba that Lieutenant Pershing earned a Silver Citation Star for his Spanish Campaign Medal, the Silver Star Medal was not yet in existence. For his service in the Philippines, then Captain Pershing was recommended for promotion to Brigadier General.[11] The system of awards and decorations in the military was still in its infancy and brevet promotions for outstanding service where still very much a part of the American military.[12] His military career also brought Pershing to Oklahoma City for a short time as Assistant Chief of Staff of the Southwest Division in 1904. Pershing would go on to serve as Commander of the American Expeditionary Force in WWI and Army Chief of Staff in 1921. He even visited Oklahoma members of the newly formed 45th Infantry Division at Camp Wolf adjacent to Fort Sill shortly before his retirement.[13] Pershing held the rank of General of the Armies when he retired in 1924, thus making him the only person to be bestowed that rank while living.[14]

One never knows what may await them in the archives of the various Masonic Bodies across the land, some truly contain hidden treasures. Even if that stack of papers in the back room does not yield up that rare signature or those rusty old swords in the armory do not bear a notable name, the fellowship is always well worth the distance traveled and a treasure unto itself.

Notes

[1] Norman Lodge No. 5 AF&AM, Tyler's Register, 1898 – 1901, Private Collection, Norman Lodge No. 38, Norman, Oklahoma.

[2] "Fort Sill," Oklahoma Historical Society's Encyclopedia of Oklahoma History and Culture, <http://digital.library.okstate.edu/encyclopedia/entries/f/fo038.html>, Accessed 6 April 2011.

[3] *The Oklahoma Consistory* (January 1918), Vol. 3, No. 1.

[4] Fort Sill Masonic Club, Memorial Plaque, Post Chapel, Fort Sill, Oklahoma.

[5] Ewell Lewis Head, Photos, 1897 – 1936, Private Collection, David Greenshields, Stillwater, Oklahoma.

[6] Robert G. Davis and James T. Tresner II, *Indians, Cowboys, Cornerstones, and Charities: A Centennial Celebration of Freemasonry in Oklahoma* (Guthrie: The Most Worshipful Grand Lodge of the State of Oklahoma Library and Museum, 2009), 156 – 161.

[7] Department of the Army, *Official Army Register: January 1951* (Washington, D.C.: Government Printing Office, 1951), Vol. 1: 514.

[8] William R. Denslow, *10,000 Famous Freemasons* (Richmond: Macoy Publishing & Masonic Supply Co., 1957), Vol. 3: 331.

[9] "John Joseph Pershing, General of the Armies," Arlington National Cemetery Website, <http://www.arlingtoncemetery.net/johnjose.htm>, Accessed 6 April 2011.

[10] Denslow, 331.

[11] "John Joseph Pershing, General of the Armies."

[12] William W. Savage, Jr., Class Lecture Notes, US Military History to 1902, University of Oklahoma, Fall, 2005.

[13] Larry Johnson, *Historic Photos of Oklahoma* (Nashville: Turner Publishing Co., 2009), 105.

[14] "John Joseph Pershing, General of the Armies."